W9-BCN-636

Global Warming: A Very Short Introduction

VERY SHORT INTRODUCTIONS are for anyone wanting a stimulating and accessible way in to a new subject. They are written by experts, and have been published in more than 25 languages worldwide.

The series began in 1995, and now represents a wide variety of topics in history, philosophy, religion, science, and the humanities. Over the next few years it will grow to a library of around 200 volumes – a Very Short Introduction to everything from ancient Egypt and Indian philosophy to conceptual art and cosmology.

Very Short Introductions available now:

ANARCHISM   Colin Ward
ANCIENT EGYPT   Ian Shaw
ANCIENT PHILOSOPHY
  Julia Annas
ANCIENT WARFARE
  Harry Sidebottom
THE ANGLO-SAXON AGE
  John Blair
ANIMAL RIGHTS
  David DeGrazia
ARCHAEOLOGY   Paul Bahn
ARCHITECTURE
  Andrew Ballantyne
ARISTOTLE   Jonathan Barnes
ART HISTORY   Dana Arnold
ART THEORY   Cynthia Freeland
THE HISTORY OF
  ASTRONOMY   Michael Hoskin
ATHEISM   Julian Baggini
AUGUSTINE   Henry Chadwick
BARTHES   Jonathan Culler
THE BIBLE   John Riches
BRITISH POLITICS
  Anthony Wright
BUDDHA   Michael Carrithers
BUDDHISM   Damien Keown
CAPITALISM   James Fulcher
THE CELTS   Barry Cunliffe
CHOICE THEORY
  Michael Allingham
CHRISTIAN ART   Beth Williamson

CHRISTIANITY   Linda Woodhead
CLASSICS   Mary Beard and
  John Henderson
CLAUSEWITZ   Michael Howard
THE COLD WAR   Robert McMahon
CONTINENTAL PHILOSOPHY
  Simon Critchley
COSMOLOGY   Peter Coles
CRYPTOGRAPHY
  Fred Piper and Sean Murphy
DADA AND SURREALISM
  David Hopkins
DARWIN   Jonathan Howard
DEMOCRACY   Bernard Crick
DESCARTES   Tom Sorell
DRUGS   Leslie Iversen
THE EARTH   Martin Redfern
EGYPTIAN MYTH   Geraldine Pinch
EIGHTEENTH-CENTURY
  BRITAIN   Paul Langford
EMOTION   Dylan Evans
EMPIRE   Stephen Howe
ENGELS   Terrell Carver
ETHICS   Simon Blackburn
THE EUROPEAN UNION
  John Pinder
EVOLUTION
  Brian and Deborah Charlesworth
FASCISM   Kevin Passmore
THE FRENCH REVOLUTION
  William Doyle

STUART BRITAIN   John Morrill
TERRORISM   Charles Townshend
THEOLOGY   David F. Ford
THE TUDORS   John Guy

TWENTIETH-CENTURY
   BRITAIN   Kenneth O. Morgan
WITTGENSTEIN   A. C. Grayling
WORLD MUSIC   Philip Bohlman

## Available soon:

AFRICAN HISTORY
   John Parker and Richard Rathbone
THE BRAIN   Michael O'Shea
BUDDHIST ETHICS
   Damien Keown
CHAOS   Leonard Smith
CITIZENSHIP   Richard Bellamy
CLASSICAL ARCHITECTURE
   Robert Tavernor
CLONING   Arlene Judith Klotzko
CONSCIOUSNESS   Sue Blackmore
CONTEMPORARY ART
   Julian Stallabrass
THE CRUSADES
   Christopher Tyerman
DERRIDA   Simon Glendinning
DESIGN   John Heskett
DINOSAURS   David Norman
DREAMING   J. Allan Hobson
ECONOMICS   Partha Dasgupta
THE ELEMENTS   Philip Ball
THE END OF THE WORLD
   Bill McGuire
EXISTENTIALISM   Thomas Flynn
FEMINISM   Margaret Walters
THE FIRST WORLD WAR
   Michael Howard
FOUCAULT   Garry Gutting
FUNDAMENTALISM
   Malise Ruthven

HABERMAS   Gordon Finlayson
HIROSHIMA
   B. R. Tomlinson
HUMAN EVOLUTION
   Bernard Wood
INTERNATIONAL RELATIONS
   Paul Wilkinson
JAZZ   Brian Morton
MANDELA   Tom Lodge
THE MIND   Martin Davies
MODERN ART   David Cottington
NATIONALISM   Steven Grosby
PERCEPTION   Richard Gregory
PHILOSOPHY OF RELIGION
   Jack Copeland and Diane Proudfoot
PHOTOGRAPHY   Steve Edwards
THE RAJ   Denis Judd
THE RENAISSANCE
   Jerry Brotton
RENAISSANCE ART
   Geraldine Johnson
ROMAN EMPIRE
   Christopher Kelly
SARTRE   Christina Howells
THE SPANISH CIVIL WAR
   Helen Graham
TIME   Leofranc Holford-Strevens
TRAGEDY   Adrian Poole
THE TWENTIETH CENTURY
   Martin Conway

For more information visit our web site
www.oup.co.uk/vsi

Mark Maslin

# GLOBAL WARMING

## A Very Short Introduction

OXFORD
UNIVERSITY PRESS

# OXFORD

UNIVERSITY PRESS

Great Clarendon Street, Oxford O X 2 6 D P

Oxford University Press is a department of the University of Oxford.
It furthers the University's objective of excellence in research, scholarship,
and education by publishing worldwide in

Oxford New York

Auckland Bangkok Buenos Aires Cape Town Chennai
Dar es Salaam Delhi Hong Kong Istanbul Karachi Kolkata
Kuala Lumpur Madrid Melbourne Mexico City Mumbai Nairobi
São Paulo Shanghai Taipei Tokyo Toronto

Oxford is a registered trade mark of Oxford University Press
in the UK and in certain other countries

Published in the United States
by Oxford University Press Inc., New York

© Mark Maslin 2004

The moral rights of the author have been asserted

Database right Oxford University Press (maker)

First published as a Very Short Introduction 2004

All rights reserved. No part of this publication may be reproduced,
stored in a retrieval system, or transmitted, in any form or by any means,
without the prior permission in writing of Oxford University Press,
or as expressly permitted by law, or under terms agreed with the appropriate
reprographics rights organizations. Enquiries concerning reproduction
outside the scope of the above should be sent to the Rights Department,
Oxford University Press, at the address above

You must not circulate this book in any other binding or cover
and you must impose this same condition on any acquirer

British Library Cataloguing in Publication Data

Data available

Library of Congress Cataloging in Publication Data

Data available

ISBN 13: 978-0-19-284097-4
ISBN 10: 0-19-284097-5

5 7 9 10 8 6

Typeset by RefineCatch Ltd, Bungay, Suffolk
Printed in Great Britain by
Ashford Colour Press Ltd, Gosport.

# Contents

# Acknowledgements

The author would like to thank the following people: Johanna and Alexandra Maslin for being there; Emma Simmons and Marsha Filion for their excellent editing and skill of finally extracting the book from me; Catherine D'Alton and Elanor McBay of the Department of Geography Drawing Office UCL; John Adams for helping me develop my critical view of this debate; Richard Betts and Eric Wolff for their insightful and extremely helpful reviews; and all my colleagues in climatology, palaeoclimatology, social science, and economics who continue to strive to understand and predict our influence on climate.

# Abbreviations

| | |
|---|---|
| AABW | Antarctic Bottom Water |
| AO | Arctic Oscillation |
| AOGCM | Atmosphere–Ocean General Circulation Models |
| AOSIS | Alliance of Small Island States |
| BINGO | Business and Industry Non-Governmental Organization |
| CFCs | chlorofluorocarbons |
| COP | Conference of the Parties |
| ENGO | Environmental Non-Governmental Organization |
| ENSO | El Niño-Southern Oscillation |
| GCM | general circulation model |
| GCR | galactic cosmic ray |
| GHCM | Global Historical Climate Network |
| IPCC | Intergovernmental Panel on Climate Change |
| JUSSCANNZ | Japan, USA, Switzerland, Canada, Australia, Norway and New Zealand |
| MAT | marine air temperature |
| NADW | North Atlantic deep water |
| NAO | North Atlantic Oscillation |
| NGO | Non-Governmental Organization |
| NRC | National Research Council |
| OECD | Organization for Economic Cooperation and Development |
| OPEC | Organization of Petroleum Exporting Countries |
| ppbv | parts per billion by volume |
| ppmv | parts per million by volume |

| | |
|---|---|
| SST | sea-surface temperature |
| THC | Thermohaline Circulation |
| UNCTAD | United Nations Conference on Trade and Development |
| UNFCCC | United Nations Framework Convention on Climate Change |
| VBD | vector-borne disease |

# List of illustrations

## Credits

1.  Intergovernmental Panel on Climate Change, *Climate Change 2001: The Scientific Basis*, (Cambridge University Press, 2001), fig. 1.2, 90, from Kiehl & Trenberth, 'Earth's Annual Mean Energy Budget', *Bulletin of the American Meteorological Society*, 78 (1997), 197–208

2.  Petit, J.R. et al., 'Climate and atmospheric history of the past 420,000 years from the Vostok Ice Core, Antarctica', *Nature*, 399 (1999), 429–36. By permission of PAGES

3.  IPPC, *Climate Change 2001: The Scientific Basis* (CUP, 2001, fig. 2, 6

4 (a & b).  © Change information kit, UNEP IUC, 1997

5.  © Mark Maslin

6.  © The Met Office, British Crown Copyright

7.  © Anabela Carvalho

8, 9, 10.   Adams, J., *Risk* (UCL Press, 1995), fig. 3.1, 34. Ibid, fig. 3.2, 35. Ibid, fig. 3.3, 37

11.  © Mark Maslin

12.  Wilson, R.C.W. et al, *The Great Ice Age* (Routledge/Open University, 2000), fig. 6.1, 114. Fig. a: IPCC, from Houghton, J.T. et al, *Climate Change: the IPCC Scientific Assessment* (CUP, 1990); figs. b-f: Duff, P., *Principles of Physical Geology* (Edward Arnold, 1994). Reproduced by permission of Hodder Arnold

13.  IPPC, *Climate Change 2001: The Scientific Basis* (CUP, 2001), fig. 5, 29

14.  Hansen, J. & Lebedeff, S., 'Global trends of measured surface air temperature', *Journal of Geophysical Research*, 92 (1987), 13345–13372. © 2004 American Geophysical Union. Reproduced by permission of AGU

15.   IPCC, Nichols, N., et al, 'Observed climate variability and change', in Houghton, J.T. et al, *Climate Change 1995: The Science of Climate Change* (CUP, 1996), 133–192

16.   IPPC, *Climate Change 2001: The Scientific Basis* (CUP, 2001), fig. 11.10, 666

17.   © Reuters/Corbis

19.   IPPC, *Climate Change 2001: The Scientific Basis* (CUP, 2001), fig. 4, 11

20.   Ibid, figs. 7a, 7b, 35

21.   IPPC, *Climate Change 2001: Impact, Adaptation and Vulnerability* (CUP, 2001), fig. SPM-1, 4

22.   IPPC, *Climate Change 2001: The Scientific Basis* (CUP, 2001), box 3, fig. 1, 48

23.   *www.climatearth.org/vital.13.htm*

24.   *IPPC Climate Change 2001: The Scientific Basis* (CUP, 2001), fig. 9, 37

25.   Ibid, fig. 5, 14

26.   © Reuters/Corbis

27.   Wilson *et al.*, *The Great Ice Age* (Routledge)

28.   Drake, F., *Global Warming* (Arnold and Oxford University Press USA, 2000). Reproduced by permission of Hodder Arnold; after Duxbury, A.C. & Duxbury, A.B., *An Introduction to the World's Oceans* (Wm. C. Crown)

29.   Seidov et al, 'The Oceans and Rapid Climate Change, Past, Present and Future', *Geophysical Monograph*, 126 (2001), fig. 3. © 2004 American Geophysical Union. Reproduced by permission of AGU

30.   Ibid, Fig. 11

31.   © Mark Maslin

32.   © Met office, British Crown Copyright

33.   Lomborg, B., *The Skeptical Environmentalist: Measuring the Real State of the World* (CUP, 2001), from Nordhaus, W. & Boyer, J., *Roll the DICE Again: Economic Models of Global Warming* (MIT Press, 2000), and Bureau of Economic Analysis, *National Income and Product Accounts* (BEA, 2001)

34.   IPPC, *Climate Change 2001: Impact, Adaptation and Vulnerability* (CUP, 2001), fig. TS-12, 71

35.  Lomborg, B., *The Skeptical Environmentalist: Measuring the Real State of the World* (CUP, 2001), from Wigley, T.M.L., 'The Kyoto Protocol', *Geophysical Research Letters* 25/13, 2,285–8, and Lee, H. et al, 'The OECD Green Model: an Updated Overview', Technical Paper, 97 (1994)

36.  Adapted from *IPPC Climate Change* (Cambridge University Press)

37.  Adapted from *IPPC Climate Change* (Cambridge University Press)

38.  © C. D'Alton

The publisher and the author apologize for any errors or omissions in the above list. If contacted they will be pleased to rectify these at the earliest opportunity.

# Introduction

Global warming is one of the most controversial science issues of the 21st century, challenging the very structure of our global society. The problem is that global warming is not just a scientific concern, but encompasses economics, sociology, geopolitics, local politics, and individuals' choice of lifestyle. Global warming is caused by the massive increase of greenhouse gases, such as carbon dioxide, in the atmosphere, resulting from the burning of fossil fuels and deforestation. There is clear evidence that we have already elevated concentrations of atmospheric carbon dioxide to their highest level for the last half million years and maybe even longer. Scientists believe that this is causing the Earth to warm faster than at any other time during, at the very least, the past one thousand years. The most recent report by the Intergovernmental Panel on Climate Change (IPCC), amounting to 2,600 pages of detailed review and analysis of published research, declares that the scientific uncertainties of global warming are essentially resolved. This report states that there is clear evidence for a 0.6°C rise in global temperatures and 20 cm rise in sea level during the 20th century. The IPCC synthesis also predicts that global temperatures could rise by between 1.4°C and 5.8°C and sea level could rise by between 20 cm and 88 cm by the year 2100. In addition, weather patterns will become less predictable and the occurrence of extreme climate events, such as storms, floods, and droughts, will increase.

This book tries to unpick the controversies that surround the global warming hypothesis and hopefully provides an incentive to read more on the subject. It starts with an explanation of global warming and climate change and is followed by a review of how the global warming hypothesis was developed. The book will also investigate why people have such extreme views about global warming, views which reflect both how people view nature and their own political agenda.

The second half of the book examines the evidence showing that global warming has already occurred and the science of predicting climate change in the future. The potentially devastating effects of global warming on human society are examined, including drastic changes in health, agriculture, the economy, water resources, coastal regions, storms and other extreme climate events, and biodiversity. For each of these areas scientists and social scientists have made estimates of the potential direct impacts; for example, it is predicted that by 2025 five billion people will experience water stress. The most important impacts are discussed in this book, along with plans to mitigate the worst of them.

There are also potential surprises that the global climate system might have in store for us, exacerbating future climate change. These include the very real possibility that global deep-ocean circulation could alter, plunging Europe into a succession of extremely cold winters or causing unprecedented global rise in sea level. There are predictions that global warming may cause vast areas of the Amazon rainforest to burn, adding extra carbon to the atmosphere and thus accelerating global warming. Finally, there is a deadly threat lurking underneath the oceans: huge reserves of methane which could be released if the oceans warm up sufficiently – again accelerating global warming. The final chapters look at global politics and potential adaptations to global warming. It should be realized that the cost of significantly cutting fossil-fuel emissions may be too expensive in the short term and hence the global economy will have to become more flexible and thus adapt to climate change. We will also have to prioritize which parts of our global environment to protect. The theory of global warming thus challenges our current concepts of the nation-state versus global responsibility, and the short-term vision of our political leaders, both of which must be overcome if global warming is to be dealt with effectively. Be under no illusion: if global warming is not taken seriously, it will be the poorest people in our global community, as usual, that suffer most.

# Chapter 1
# **What is global warming?**

## The Earth's natural greenhouse

The temperature of the Earth is controlled by the balance between
the input from energy of the sun and the loss of this back into space.
Certain atmospheric gases are critical to this temperature balance
and are known as greenhouse gases. The energy received from
the sun is in the form of short-wave radiation, i.e. in the visible
spectrum and ultraviolet radiation. On average, about one-third of
this solar radiation that hits the Earth is reflected back to space.
Of the remainder, some is absorbed by the atmosphere, but most
is absorbed by the land and oceans. The Earth's surface becomes
warm and as a result emits long-wave 'infrared' radiation. The
greenhouse gases trap and re-emit some of this long-wave
radiation, and warm the atmosphere. Naturally occurring
greenhouse gases include water vapour, carbon dioxide, ozone,
methane, and nitrous oxide, and together they create a natural
greenhouse or blanket effect, warming the Earth by 35°C. Despite
the greenhouse gases often being depicted in diagrams as one layer,
this is only to demonstrate their 'blanket effect', as they are in fact
mixed throughout the atmosphere (see Figure 1).

Another way to understand the Earth's natural 'greenhouse' is by
comparing it to its two nearest neighbours. A planet's climate is
decided by several factors: its mass, its distance from the sun, and of
course the composition of its atmosphere and in particular the

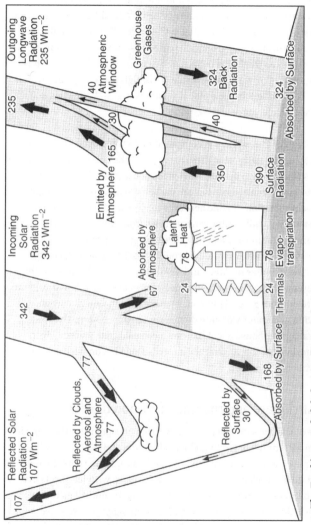

1. The Earth's annual global mean energy balance

amount of greenhouse gases. For example, the planet Mars is very small, and therefore its gravity is too small to retain a dense atmosphere; its atmosphere is about a hundred times thinner than Earth's and consists mainly of carbon dioxide. Mars's average surface temperature is about –50°C, so what little carbon dioxide exists is frozen in the ground. In comparison, Venus has almost the same mass as the Earth but a much denser atmosphere, which is composed of 96% carbon dioxide. This high percentage of carbon dioxide produces intense global warming and so Venus has a surface temperature of over + 460°C.

The Earth's atmosphere is composed of 78% nitrogen, 21% oxygen, and 1% other gases. It is these other gases that we are interested in, as they include the so-called greenhouse gases. The two most important greenhouse gases are carbon dioxide and water vapour. Currently, carbon dioxide accounts for just 0.03–0.04% of the atmosphere, while water vapour varies from 0 to 2%. Without the natural greenhouse effect that these two gases produce, the Earth's average temperature would be roughly –20°C. The comparison with the climates on Mars and Venus is very stark because of the different thicknesses of their atmospheres and the relative amounts of greenhouse gases. However, because the amount of carbon dioxide and water vapour can vary on Earth, we know that this natural greenhouse effect has produced a climate system which is naturally unstable and rather unpredictable in comparison to those of Mars and Venus.

## Past climate and the role of carbon dioxide

One of the ways in which we know that atmospheric carbon dioxide is important in controlling global climate is through the study of our past climate. Over the last two and half million years the Earth's climate has cycled between the great ice ages, with ice sheets over 3 km thick over North America and Europe, to conditions that were even milder than they are today. These changes are extremely rapid if compared to other geological variations, such as the movement of continents around the globe, where we are looking at a time period of millions of years. But how do we know about these massive ice ages and the role of carbon dioxide? The evidence mainly comes from ice cores drilled in both Antarctica and Greenland. As snow falls, it is light and fluffy and contains a lot of air. When this is slowly compacted to form ice, some of this air is trapped. By extracting these air bubbles trapped in the ancient ice, scientists can measure the percentage of greenhouse gases that were present in the past atmosphere. Scientists have drilled over two miles down into both the Greenland and Antarctic ice sheets, which has enabled them to reconstruct the amount of greenhouse gases that occurred in the atmosphere over the last half a million years. By examining the oxygen and hydrogen isotopes in the ice core, it is possible to estimate the temperature at which the ice was formed. The results are striking, as greenhouse gases such as atmospheric carbon dioxide ($CO_2$) and methane ($CH_4$) co-vary with temperatures over the last 400,000 years (see Figure 2). This strongly supports the

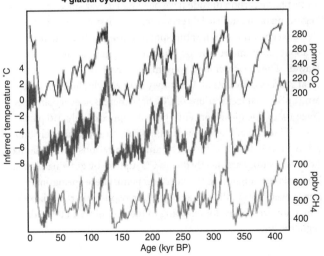

4 glacial cycles recorded in the Vostok ice core

2. Greenhouse gases and temperature for the last four glacial cycles recorded in the Vostok ice core

idea that the carbon dioxide content in the atmosphere and global temperature are closely linked, i.e. when $CO_2$ and $CH_4$ increase, the temperature is found to increase and vice versa. This is our greatest concern for future climate: if levels of greenhouse gases continue to rise, so will the temperature of our atmosphere. The study of past climate, as we will see throughout this book, provides many clues about what could happen in the future. One of the most worrying results from the study of ice cores, and lake and deep-sea sediments, is that past climate has varied regionally by at least 5°C in a few decades, suggesting that climate follows a non-linear path. Hence we should expect sudden and dramatic surprises when greenhouse gas levels reach an as yet unknown trigger point in the future.

## The rise in atmospheric carbon dioxide during the industrial period

One of the few areas of the global warming debate which seems to be universally accepted is that there is clear proof that levels of atmospheric carbon dioxide have been rising ever since the beginning of the industrial revolution. The first measurements of $CO_2$ concentrations in the atmosphere started in 1958 at an altitude of about 4,000 metres on the summit of Mauna Loa mountain in Hawaii. The measurements were made here to be remote from local sources of pollution. What they have clearly shown is that atmospheric concentrations of $CO_2$ have increased every single year since 1958. The mean concentration of approximately 316 parts per million by volume (ppmv) in 1958 rose to approximately 369 ppmv in 1998 (see Figure 3). The annual variations in the Mauna Loa observatory are mostly due to $CO_2$ uptake by growing plants. The uptake is highest in the northern hemisphere springtime; hence every spring there is a drop in atmospheric carbon dioxide which unfortunately does nothing to the overall trend towards ever higher values.

This carbon dioxide data from the Mauna Loa observatory can be combined with the detailed work on ice cores to produce a complete

## (a) Global atmospheric concentrations of three well mixed greenhouse gases

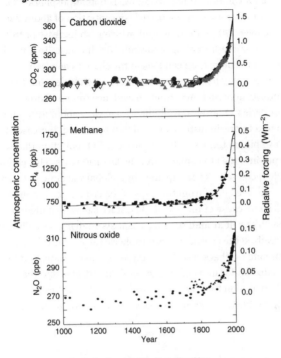

## (b) Sulphate aerosols deposited in Greenland ice

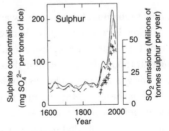

3. Indicators of the human influence on the atmosphere composition during the industrial era

record of atmospheric carbon dioxide since the beginning of the industrial revolution. What this shows is that atmospheric $CO_2$ has increased from a pre-industrial concentration of about 280 ppmv to over 370 ppmv at present, which is an increase of 160 billion tonnes, representing an overall 30% increase. To put this increase into context, we can look at the changes between the last ice age, when temperatures were much lower, and the pre-industrial period. According to evidence from ice cores, atmospheric $CO_2$ levels during the ice age were about 200 ppmv compared to pre-industrial levels of 280 ppmv – an increase of over 160 billion tonnes – almost the same $CO_2$ pollution that we have put into the atmosphere over the last 100 years. This carbon dioxide increase was accompanied by a global warming of 6°C as the world freed itself from the grips of the last ice age. Though the ultimate cause of the end of the last ice age was changes in the Earth's orbit around the sun, scientists studying past climates have realized the central role atmospheric carbon dioxide has as a climate feedback translating these external variations into the waxing and waning of ice ages. It demonstrates that the level of pollution that we have already caused in one century is comparable to the natural variations which took thousands of years.

## The enhanced greenhouse effect

The debate surrounding the global warming hypothesis is whether the additional greenhouse gases being added to the atmosphere will enhance the natural greenhouse effect. Global warming sceptics argue that though levels of carbon dioxide in the atmosphere are rising, this will not cause global warming, as either the effects are too small or there are other natural feedbacks which will counter major warming. Even if one takes the view of the majority of scientists and accepts that burning fossil fuels will cause warming, there is a different debate over exactly how much temperatures will increase. Then there is the discussion about whether global climate will respond in a linear manner to the extra greenhouse gases or whether there is a climate threshold waiting for us. These issues are tackled later in the book.

## Who produces the pollution?

The United Nations Framework Convention on Climate Change was created to produce the first international agreement on reducing global greenhouse gas emissions. However, this task is not as simple as it first appears, as carbon dioxide emissions are not evenly produced by countries. The first major source of carbon dioxide is the burning of fossil fuels, since a significant part of carbon dioxide emissions comes from energy production, industrial processes, and transport. These are not evenly distributed around the world because of the unequal distribution of industry; hence, any agreement would affect certain countries' economies more than others. Consequently, at the moment, the industrialized countries must bear the main responsibility for reducing emissions of carbon dioxide to about 22 billion tonnes of carbon per year (see Figure 4a). North America, Europe, and Asia emit over 90% of the global industrially produced carbon dioxide. Moreover, historically they have emitted much more than less-developed countries.

The second major source of carbon dioxide emissions is as a result of land-use changes. These emissions come primarily from the cutting down of forests for the purposes of agriculture, urbanization, or roads. When large areas of rainforests are cut down, the land often turns into less productive grasslands with considerably less capacity for storing $CO_2$. Here the pattern of carbon dioxide emissions is different, with South America, Asia, and Africa being responsible for over 90% of present-day land-use change emissions, about 4 billion tonnes of carbon per year (see Figure 4b). This, though, should be viewed against the historical fact that North America and Europe had already changed their own landscape by the beginning of the 20th century. In terms of the amount of carbon dioxide released, industrial processes still significantly outweigh land-use changes.

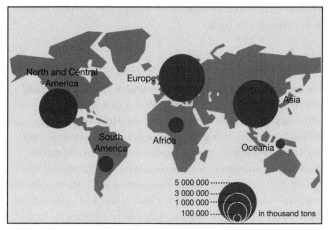

**4a. CO₂ emissions from industrial processes**

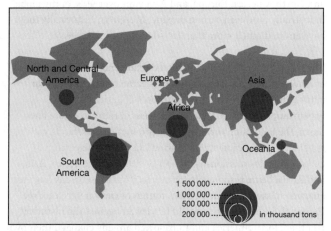

**4b. CO₂ emissions from land-use change**

So who are the bad guys in causing this increase in atmospheric carbon dioxide? Of course, it is the developed countries who historically have emitted most of the anthropogenic (man-made) greenhouse gases, as they have been emitting since the start of the industrial revolution in the latter half of the 1700s. Moreover, a mature industrialized economy is energy-hungry and burns vast quantities of fossil fuels. A major issue in the continuing debate is the sharing of responsibility. Non-industrialized countries are striving to increase their population's standard of living, thereby also increasing their emissions of greenhouse gases, since economic development is closely associated with energy production. The volume of carbon dioxide thus will probably increase, despite the efforts to reduce emissions in industrialized countries. For example, China has the second biggest emissions of carbon dioxide in the world. However, per capita the Chinese emissions are ten times lower than those of the USA, who are top of the list. So this means that in the USA every person is responsible for producing ten times more carbon dioxide pollution than in China. So all the draft international agreements concerning cutting emissions since the Rio Earth Summit in 1992 have for moral reasons not included the developing world, as this is seen as an unfair brake on its economic development. However, this is a significant issue because, for example, both China and India are rapidly industrializing, and with a combined population of over 2.3 billion people they will produce a huge amount of pollution.

## What is the IPCC?

The Intergovernmental Panel on Climate Change (IPCC) was established in 1988 jointly by the United Nations Environmental Panel and World Meteorological Organization because of worries about the possibility of global warming. The purpose of the IPCC is the continued assessment of the state of knowledge on the various aspects of climate change, including scientific, environmental, and socio-economic impacts and response strategies. The IPCC is recognized as the most authoritative scientific and technical voice on climate change, and its assessments have had a profound influence on the negotiators of the United Nations Framework Convention on Climate Change (UNFCCC) and its Kyoto Protocol. The meetings in The Hague in November 2000 and in Bonn in July 2001 were the second and third attempts to ratify (i.e. to make legal) the Protocols laid out in Kyoto in 1998. Unfortunately, President Bush pulled the USA out of the negotiations in March 2001. However, 186 other countries made history in July 2001 by agreeing the most far-reaching and comprehensive environmental treaty the world has ever seen. But the Kyoto Protocol has yet to be ratified. What is required for this to happen is discussed in Chapter 8.

The IPCC is organized into three working groups plus a task force to calculate the amount of greenhouse gases produced by each country. Each of these four bodies has two co-chairmen (one from a developed and one from a developing country) and a technical support unit. Working Group I assesses the scientific aspects of the climate system and climate change; Working Group II addresses the vulnerability of human and natural systems to climate change, the negative and positive consequences of climate change, and options for adapting to them; and Working Group III assesses options for limiting greenhouse gas emissions and otherwise mitigating climate change, as well as economic issues. Hence the IPCC also provides governments with scientific, technical, and socio-economic information relevant to evaluating the risks and to developing a response to global climate change. The latest reports from these three working groups were published in 2001 and approximately 400 experts from some 120 countries were directly involved in drafting, revising, and finalizing the IPCC reports and another 2,500 experts participated in the review process. The IPCC authors are always nominated by governments and by international organizations including Non-Governmental Organizations. These reports are essential reading for anyone interested in global warming and are listed in the Further Reading section.

The IPCC also compiles research on the main greenhouse gases: where they come from, and the current consensus concerning their warming potential (see below). The warming potential is calculated in comparison with carbon dioxide, which is allocated a warming potential of one. This way the different greenhouse gases can be compared with each other relatively instead of in absolute terms. The Global Warming potential is calculated over a 20- and 100-year period. This is because different greenhouse gases have different residence times in the atmosphere because of how long they take to break down in the atmosphere or be absorbed in the ocean or terrestrial biosphere. Most other greenhouse gases are more effective at warming the atmosphere than carbon dioxide but are still in very low concentrations in the atmosphere. As you can see from Table 1 there are other greenhouse gases which are much more dangerous mass for mass than carbon dioxide but these exist in very low concentrations in the atmosphere, and therefore most of the debate concerning global warming still centres on the role and control of atmospheric carbon dioxide.

## What is climate change?

Many scientists believe that the human-induced or anthropogenic-enhanced greenhouse effect will cause climate change in the near future. Even some of the global warming sceptics argue that though global warming may be a minor influence, natural climate change does occur on human timescales and we should be prepared to adapt to it. But what is climate change and how does it occur? Climate change can manifest itself in a number of ways, for example changes in regional and global temperatures, changing rainfall patterns, expansion and contraction of ice sheets, and sea-level variations. These regional and global climate changes are responses to external and/or internal forcing mechanisms. An example of an internal forcing mechanism is the variations in the carbon dioxide content of the atmosphere modulating the greenhouse effect, while a good example of an external forcing mechanism is the long-term variations in the Earth's orbits around the sun, which alter the

Table 1: Main greenhouse gases and their comparative ability to warm the atmosphere

| Greenhouse gas | Chemical formula | Pre-industrial concentrations | 1994 concentrations | Human source | Global warming potential 20 years | Global warming potential 100 years |
|---|---|---|---|---|---|---|
| Carbon dioxide | $CO_2$ | 278 ppmv | 358 ppmv (30% increase) | Fossil-fuel combustion Land-use changes Cement production | 1 | 1 |
| Methane | $CH_4$ | 700 ppbv | 1721 ppbv (240% increase) | Fossil fuels Rice paddies Waste dumps Livestock | 62 | 23 |
| Nitrous oxide | $N_2O$ | 275 ppbv | 311 ppbv (15% increase) | Fertilizer Industrial processes Fossil-fuel combustion | 275 | 296 |

| | | | | | | | |
|---|---|---|---|---|---|---|---|
| CFC-12 | $CCl_2F_2$ | 0 | Does not exist naturally and is human generated | 0.503 ppbv | Liquid coolants/foams | 6200 | 7100 |
| HCFC-22 | $CHClF_2$ | 0 | Does not exist naturally and is human generated | 0.105 ppbv | Liquid coolants | 1300 | 1400 |
| Perfluoro methane | $CF_4$ | 0 | Does not exist naturally and is human generated | 0.070 ppbv | Production of aluminium | 3900 | 5700 |
| Sulphur hexa-fluoride | $SF_6$ | 0 | Does not exist naturally and is human generated | 0.032 ppbv | Dielectric fluid | 15,100 | 22,200 |

ppmv = part per million by volume
ppbv = parts per billion by volume

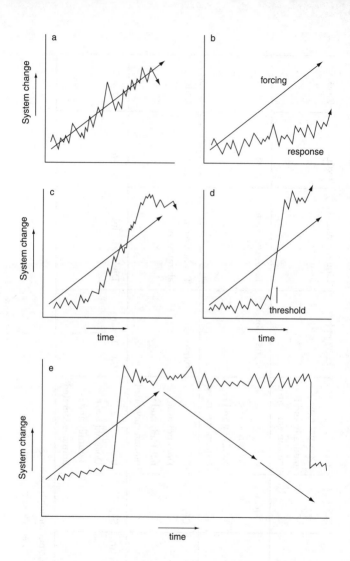

5. **Possible climate system responses to a linear-forcing**

regional distribution of solar radiation to the Earth. This is thought to cause the waxing and waning of the ice ages. So in terms of looking for the evidence for global warming and predicting the future, we need to take account of all the natural external and internal forcing mechanisms. For example, until recently the cooling that occurred globally during the 1970s was unexplained until the 'external' and cyclic variations every 11 years in the sun's energy output, the so-called sunspot cycle, was taken into consideration.

We can also try to abstract the way the global climate system responds to an internal or external forcing agent by examining different scenarios (see Figure 5). In these scenarios I am assuming that there is only one forcing mechanism which is trying to change the global climate. What is important is how the global climate system will react. For example, is the relationship like a person trying to push a car up a hill which, strangely enough, gets very little response? Or is it more like a person pushing a car downhill, which, once the car starts to move, it is very difficult to stop. There are four possible relationships and this is the central question in the global warming debate, which is most applicable to the future.

(a)  Linear and synchronous response (Figure 5a). In this case the forcing produces a direct response in the climate system whose magnitude is in proportion to the forcing. In terms of global warming an extra million tonnes of carbon dioxide would cause a certain predictable temperature increase. This can be equated to pushing a car along a flat road: most of the energy put into pushing is used to move the car forward.

(b)  Muted or limited response (Figure 5b). In this case the forcing may be strong, but the climate system is in some way buffered and therefore gives very little response. Many global warming sceptics and politicians argue that the climate system is very insensitive to changes in atmospheric carbon dioxide so very little will happen in the future. This is the 'pushing the car up the hill' analogy: you can spend as much energy as you like trying to push the car but it will not move very far.

(c) Delayed or non-linear response (Figure 5c). In this case, the climate system may have a slow response to the forcing thanks to being buffered in some way. After an initial period the climate system responds to the forcing but in a non-linear way. This is a real possibility when it comes to global warming and why it is argued that as yet only a small amount of warming has been observed over the last 100 years. This scenario can be equated to the car on the top of a hill: it takes some effort and thus time to push the car to the edge of the hill; this is the buffering effect. Once the car has reached the edge it takes very little to push the car over, and then it accelerates down the hill with or without your help. Once it reaches the bottom, the car then continues for some time, which is the overshoot, and then slows down of its own accord and settles into a new state.

(d) Threshold response (Figure 5d). In this case, initially, there is no or very little response in the climate system to the forcing; however, all the response takes place in a very short period of time in one large step or threshold. In many cases the response may be much larger than one would expect from the size of the forcing and this can be referred to as a response overshoot. This is the scenario that most worries us, as thresholds are very difficult to model and thus predict. However, thresholds have been found to be very common in the study of past climates, with rapid regional climate changes of over 5°C occurring within a few decades. This scenario equates to the bus hanging off the cliff at the end of the original film *The Italian Job*; as long as there are only very small changes, nothing happens at all. However, a critical point (in this case weight) is reached and the bus (and the gold) plunge off the cliff into the ravine below.

Though these are purely theoretical models of how the global climate system can respond, they are important to keep in mind when reviewing the possible scenarios for future climate change. Moreover, they are important when we consider in Chapter 3 why different people see different global warming futures despite all having access to the same information. It depends on which of the above scenarios they believe will happen. An added complication when assessing climate change is the possibility that climate thresholds contain bifurcations. This means the forcing required to go one way through the threshold is different from the reverse (see Figure 5e). This implies that once a climate threshold has occurred, it is a lot more difficult to reverse it. The bifurcation of the climate system has been inferred from ocean models which mimic the impact of fresh water in the North Atlantic on the global deep-water circulation, and we will discuss this can of worms in great detail in Chapter 7.

## Linking global warming with climate change

We have seen that there is clear evidence that greenhouse gas concentrations in the atmosphere have been rising since the industrial revolution in the 18th century. The current scientific consensus is that changes in greenhouse gas concentrations in the atmosphere do cause global temperature change. However, the biggest problem with the global warming hypothesis is understanding how sensitive the global climate is to increased levels of atmospheric carbon dioxide. Even if we establish this, predicting climate change is complex because it encompasses many different factors, which respond differently when the atmosphere warms up, including regional temperature changes, melting glaciers and ice sheets, relative sea-level change, precipitation changes, storm intensity and tracks, El Niño, and even ocean circulation. This linkage between global warming and climate change is further complicated by the fact that each part of the global climate system has different response times. For example, the atmosphere can respond to external or internal changes within a day, but the deep ocean may take decades to respond, while vegetation can alter its structure within a few weeks (e.g. change the amount of leaves) but its composition (e.g. swapping plant types) can take up to a century to change. Then, add to this the possibility of natural forcing which may be cyclic; for example, there is good evidence that sunspot cycles can affect climate on both a decadal and a century timescale. There is also evidence that since the beginning of our present interglacial period, the last 10,000 years, there have been climatic coolings every 1,500 ±500 years, of which the Little Ice Age was the last. The Little Ice Age began in the 17th and ended in the 18th century and was characterized by a fall of 0.5–1°C in Greenland temperatures, significant shift in the currents around Iceland, and a sea-surface temperature fall of 4°C off the coast of West Africa, 2°C off the Bermuda Rise, and of course ice fairs on the River Thames in London, all of which were due to natural climate change. So we need to disentangle natural climate variability from global warming. We need to understand how the different parts of the climate system interact, remembering that they all have different response times. We need to understand what sort of climatic change will be caused, and whether it will be gradual or catastrophic. We also need to understand how different regions of the world will be affected; for example, it is suggested that additional greenhouse gases will warm up the poles more than the tropics. All these themes concerning an understanding of the climate system and the difficulty of future climate prediction are returned to in Chapters 4 and 5.

So if you are reading this book for the first time and are primarily interested in the science of global warming then I would suggest you read Chapters 4, 5, 6, and 7. However, I would encourage you also to read Chapters 2, 3, 8, and 9, which look at the social, historic, economic, and political aspects of global warming, since global warming, as far as I am concerned, cannot be seen as a scientific problem; rather, it is a problem for our global society.

# Chapter 2
# A brief history of the global warming hypothesis

## Historical background

Scientists are predicting that global warming could warm the planet by between 1.4 and 5.8°C in the next 100 years, causing huge problems for humanity. In the face of such a threat it is essential to understand the history of the global warming theory and the evidence that supports it. Can the future really be as bleak as scientists are predicting? This whole debate over the global warming theory and its possible impacts, more than any other controversy in science, demonstrates the humanity of scientists and the politics of new scientific ideas. This is because, despite the Hollywood vision of scientists, we are not logical machines like Mr Spock from *Star Trek*, nor mad scientists like Dr Frankenstein, but highly driven individuals. Though I must admit I do like the heroic portrayal of a 'paleoclimatologist' in the *Day after Tomorrow*; if only we were really like that. So it must remembered that money is not the main driving force of science; rather it is curiosity tainted with ambition, ego, and the prospect of fame. So please divest yourself of the image of scientists divorced from the world around them. The history of the global warming hypothesis clearly shows that science is deeply influenced by society and vice versa. So what we discover is that the essential science of global warming was carried out 50 years ago under the perceived necessity of geosciences during the Cold War, but was not taken seriously as a theory until the late 1980s. I hope to give you some insight into why there was such a significant delay.

It is now over one hundred years ago that global warming was officially discovered. The pioneering work in 1896 by the Swedish scientist Svante Arrhenius, and the subsequent independent confirmation by Thomas Chamberlin, calculated that human activity could substantially warm the Earth by adding carbon dioxide to the atmosphere. This conclusion was the by-product of other research, its major aim being to offer a theory whereby decreased carbon dioxide would explain the causes of the great ice ages, a theory which still stands today but which had to wait until 1987 for the Antarctic Vostok ice-core results to confirm the pivotal role of atmospheric $CO_2$ in controlling past global climate. However, no one else took up the research topic, so both Arrhenius and Chamberlin turned to other challenges. This was because scientists at that time felt there were so many other influences on global climate, from sunspots to ocean circulation, that minor human influences were thought insignificant in comparison to the mighty forces of astronomy and geology. This idea was reinforced by research during the 1940s, which developed the theory that changes in the orbit of the Earth around the sun controlled the waxing and waning of the great ice ages. A second line of argument was that because there is 50 times more carbon dioxide in the oceans than in the atmosphere, it was conjectured that 'The sea acts as a vast equalizer', in other words the ocean would mop up our pollution.

This dismissive view took its first blow when in the 1940s there was a significant improvement in infrared spectroscopy, the technique used to measure long-wave radiation. Up until the 1940s experiments had shown that carbon dioxide did block the transmission of infrared 'long-wave' radiation of the sort given off by the Earth. However, the experiments showed there was very little change in this interception if the amount of carbon dioxide was doubled or halved. This meant that even small amounts of carbon dioxide could block radiation so thoroughly that adding more gas made very little difference. Moreover, water vapour, which is much more abundant than carbon dioxide, was found to block radiation in the same way and, therefore, was thought to be more important. The Second World War saw a massive improvement in technology and the old measurements of carbon dioxide radiation interception were revisited. In the original experiments sea-level pressure was used but it was found that at the rarefied upper atmosphere pressures the general absorption did not occur and, therefore, radiation was able to pass through the upper atmosphere and into space. This proved that increasing the amount of carbon dioxide did result in absorption of more radiation. Moreover, it was found that water vapour absorbed other types of radiation rather than carbon dioxide, and to compound it all, it was also discovered that the stratosphere, the upper atmosphere, was bone dry. This work was brought together in 1955 by the calculations of Gilbert Plass, who concluded that adding more carbon dioxide to the atmosphere would intercept more infrared radiation, preventing it being lost to space and thus warming the planet.

This still left the argument that the oceans would soak up the extra anthropogenically produced carbon dioxide. The first new evidence came in the 1950s and showed that the average lifetime of a carbon dioxide molecule in the atmosphere before it dissolved in the sea was about ten years. As the ocean overturning takes several hundreds of years, it was assumed the extra carbon dioxide would be safely locked in the oceans. But Roger Revelle (director of Scripps Institute of Oceanography in California) realized that it was necessary not only to know that a carbon dioxide molecule was absorbed after ten years but to ask what happened to it after that. Did it stay there or diffuse back into the atmosphere? How much extra $CO_2$ could the oceans hold? Revelle's calculations showed that the complexities of the surface ocean chemistry are such that it returns much of the carbon dioxide that it absorbs. This was a great revelation, and showed that because of the peculiarities of ocean chemistry, the oceans would not be the complete sink for anthropogenic carbon dioxide that was first thought. This principle still holds true, although the exact amount of anthropogenic carbon dioxide taken up per year by the oceans is still in debate. It is thought to be about 2 gigatonnes, nearly a third of the annual total anthropogenic production.

Charles Keeling, who was hired by Roger Revelle, produced the next important step forward in the global warming debate. In the late 1950s and early 1960s Keeling used the most modern technology available to measure the concentration of atmospheric $CO_2$ in Antarctica and Mauna Loa. The resulting Keeling $CO_2$ curves have continued to climb ominously each year since the first measurement in 1958 and have become one of the major icons of global warming.

Spencer Weart, the director of the Center of History of Physics at the American Institute of Physics, argues that all the scientific facts about enhanced atmospheric $CO_2$ and potential global warming were assembled by the late 1950s–early 1960s. He argues that it was only due to the physical geosciences being favoured financially in the Cold War environment that so much of the fundamental work on global warming was completed. Gilbert Plass published an article in 1959 in *Scientific American* declaring that the world's temperature would rise by 3°C by the end of the century. The magazine editors published an accompanying photograph of coal smoke belching from factories and the caption read, 'Man upsets the balance of natural processes by adding billions of tons of carbon dioxide to the atmosphere each year'. This resembles thousands of magazine articles, television news items, and documentaries that we have all seen since the late 1980s. So why was there a delay between the science of global warming being accepted and in place in the late 1950s and early 1960s and the sudden realization of the true threat of global warming during the late 1980s?

# Why did it take so long to recognize global warming?

The key reasons for the delay in recognizing the global warming threat were, first, the power of the global mean temperature data set and, second, the need for the emergence of global environmental awareness. The global mean temperature data set is calculated using the land-air and sea-surface temperature. From 1940 till the mid-1970s the global temperature curve seems to have had a general downward trend. This provoked many scientists to discuss whether the Earth was entering the next great ice age. This fear developed in part because of increased awareness in the 1970s of how variable global climate had been in the past. The emerging subject of palaeoceanography (study of past oceans) demonstrated from deep-sea sediments that there were at least 32 glacial-interglacial (cold-warm) cycles in the last two and a half million years, not four as had been previously assumed. The time resolution of these studies was low, so that there was no possibility of estimating how quickly the ice ages came and went, only how regularly. It led many scientists and the media to ignore the scientific revelations of the 1950s and 1960s in favour of global cooling. As Ponte (1976) summarized:

> Since the 1940's the northern half of our planet has been cooling rapidly. Already the effect in the United States is the same as if every city had been picked up by giant hands and set down more than 100 miles closer to the North Pole. If the cooling continues, warned the National Academy of Sciences in 1975, we could possibly witness the beginning of the next Great Ice Age. Conceivably, some of us might live to see huge snow fields remaining year-round in northern regions of the United States and Europe. Probably, we would see mass global famine in our life times, perhaps even within a decade. Since 1970, half a million human beings in northern Africa and Asia have starved because of floods and droughts caused by the cooling climate.

It was not until the early 1980s, when the global annual mean temperature curve started to increase, that the global cooling scenario was questioned. By the late 1980s the global annual mean temperature curve rose so steeply that all the dormant evidence from the late 1950s and 1960s was given prominence and the global warming theory was in full swing. What is intriguing is that some of the most vocal advocates for the global warming theory were also the ones responsible for creating concern over the impending ice age. In *The Genesis Strategy* in 1976, Stephen Schneider stressed that the global cooling trend had set in; he is now one of the leading proponents of global warming. In 1990 he stated that 'the rate of change [warming] is so fast that I don't hesitate to call that kind of change potentially catastrophic for ecosystems'.

Why the hysteria? John Gribbin (1989) describes the transition very neatly in his book *In Hothouse Earth: the Greenhouse Effect and Gaia*.

In 1981 it was possible to stand back and take a leisurely look at the record from 1880 to 1980 . . . . In 1987, the figures were updated to 1985, chiefly for neatness of adding another half a decade to the records . . . . But by early 1988, even one more year's worth of data justified another publication in April, just four months after the last 1987 measurements were made, pointing out the record-breaking warmth now being reached. Even there, Hansen [James Hansen, head of the NASA team studying global temperature trends] and Lebedeff were cautious about making the connection with the greenhouse effect, merely saying that this was 'a subject beyond the scope of this paper'. But in four months it had taken to get the 1987 data in print, the world had changed again; just a few weeks later Hansen was telling the US Senate that the first five months of 1988 had been warmer than any comparable period since 1880, and greenhouse effect was upon us.

It seems, therefore, that the whole global warming issue was driven by the upturn in the global annual mean temperature data set. This in itself is interesting because some scientists in the early 1990s believed that this was a flawed data set because: (1) many of the land monitoring stations have subsequently been surrounded by urban areas, thus increasing the temperature records because of the urban heat island effect, (2) there have been changes in the ways ships measure the sea-water temperature, (3) there was not an adequate explanation for the cooling trend in the 1970s, (4) satellite data did not show a warming trend from the 1970s to the 1990s, and (5) the global warming models have overestimated the warming that should have occurred in the northern hemisphere over the last 100 years. Since the early 1990s the urban heat island and variations in sea-temperature measurements have been taken into account. We now know that the cooling trend of the 1970s is due to the decadal influence of the sunspot cycle. It turns out that the satellite results were spurious for a number of reasons and a greater understanding of the system and recalibrated data shows a significant warming trend. Lastly, it was discovered that other pollutants, such as sulphur dioxide aerosols, have been cooling industrial regions of the globe, and as the models of the early 1990s did not take them into consideration, they were overestimating the amount of warming. So the latest IPCC 2001 Science Report has reviewed and synthesized a wide range of data sets and shows that, essentially, the trend in the temperature data is correct, and that this warming trend has continued unstopped until the present day (see Figure 6). In fact we know that 1998 was globally the warmest year on record, with 2002 the second, 2003 the third, 2001 the fourth and 1997 the fifth warmest. Indeed the ten warmest years on record have all occurred since 1990.

The upturn in the global annual mean temperature data was not the sole reason for the appearance of the global warming issue. During the 1980s there was also an intense drive to understand past climate change. Major advances were made in obtaining high-resolution past climate records from deep-sea sediments and ice cores. It was, thus, realized that glacial periods, or ice ages, take tens of thousand years to occur, primarily because ice sheets are very slow to build up

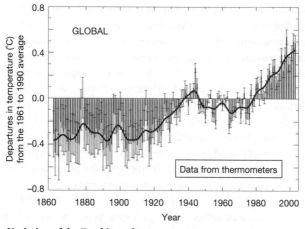

**6. Variation of the Earth's surface temperature**

and are naturally unstable. In contrast, the transition to a warmer period or interglacial, such as the present, is geologically very quick, in the order of a couple of thousand years. This is because once the ice sheets start to melt there are a number of positive feedbacks that accelerate the process, such as sea-level rise, which can undercut and destroy large ice sheets. The realization occurred in the palaeoclimate community that global warming is much easier and more rapid than cooling. It also put to rest the myth of the next impending ice age. As the glacial-interglacial periods of the last two and half million years have been shown to be forced by the changes in the orbit of the Earth around the sun, it would be possible to predict when the next glacial period will begin, if there were no anthropogenic effects involved. According to the model predictions by Berger and Loutre (2002) at the Université catholique de Louvain in Belgium, we do not need to worry about another ice age for at least 5,000 years. Indeed, if their model is correct and atmospheric carbon dioxide concentrations double, then global warming would postpone the next ice age for another 45,000 years. Palaeoclimate work has also provided us with worrying insights into how the climate system works. Recent work on the ice cores and deep-sea sediments demonstrate that at least regional climate changes of 5°C can occur in a matter of decades. This work on reconstructing past climate seems to demonstrate that the global climate system is not benign but highly dynamic and prone to rapid changes.

The next change that occurred during the 1980s was a massive grass-roots expansion in the environmental movement, particularly in the USA, Canada, and the UK, partly as a backlash against the right-wing governments of the 1980s and the expansion of the consumer economy and partly because of the increasing number of environmental-related stories in the media. This heralded a new era of global environmental awareness and transnational NGOs (Non-Governmental Organizations). The roots of this growing environmental awareness can be traced back to a number of key markers; these include the publication of Rachel Carson's *Silent Spring* in 1962, the image of Earth seen from the moon in 1969, the Club of Rome's 1972 report on *Limits to Growth*, the Three Mile Island nuclear reactor accident in 1979, the nuclear accident at Chernobyl in 1986, and the *Exxon Valdez* oil spillage in 1989. But these environmental problems were all regional in effect, i.e. limited geographically to the specific area in which they occurred.

It was the discovery in 1985 by the British Antarctic Survey of depletion of ozone over Antarctica which demonstrated the global connectivity of our environment. The ozone 'hole' also had a tangible international cause, the use of CFCs, which led to a whole new area of politics, the international management of the environment. There followed a set of key agreements, the 1985 Vienna Convention for the Protection of the Ozone Layer, the 1987 Montreal Protocol on Substances that Deplete the Ozone layer, and the 1990 London and 1992 Copenhagen Adjustments and Amendments to the Protocol. These have been held up as examples of successful environmental diplomacy. Climate change has had a slower development in international politics and far less has been

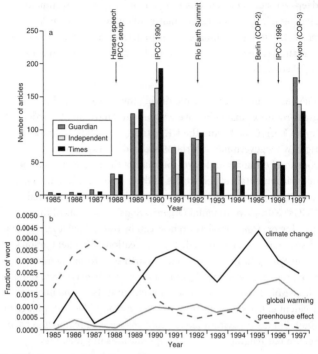

7. **Global warming and the media**

achieved in terms of regulation and implementation. This is, at its most simplistic level, because of the great inherent uncertainties of the science and the greater economic costs involved.

The other reason for the acceptance of the global warming hypothesis was the intense media interest throughout the late 1980s and 1990s. This is because the global warming hypothesis was perfect for the media: a dramatic story about the end of the world as we know it, with important controversy about whether it was even true. Anabela Carvalho, now at the University of Minho (Braga, Portugal), has done a fascinating study of the British quality press coverage of the global warming issue between 1985 and 1997. She concentrated particularly on the *Guardian* and *The Times* and found throughout this period that they promoted very different world-views. Interestingly, despite their differing views, the number of articles published per year by the British quality (broadsheet) papers followed a similar pattern and peaked when there were key IPCC reports published or international conferences on climate change (see Figure 7). But it is the nature of these articles that shows how the global warming debate was constructed in the media. From the late 1980s *The Times*, which published most articles on global warming in 1989, 1990, and 1992, cast doubt on the claims of climate change. There was a recurrent attempt to promote mistrust in science, through strategies of generalization, of disagreement within the scientific community, and, most importantly, discrediting scientists and scientific institutions. A very similar viewpoint was taken by the majority of the American media throughout much of the 1990s. In fact it has been claimed that this approach in the American media has led to a barrier between scientists and the public in the USA. In the UK the *Guardian* newspaper took the opposite approach to that of *The Times*. Although the *Guardian* gave space to the technical side of the debate, it soon started to discuss scientific claims in the wider context. As scientific uncertainty regarding the enhanced greenhouse effect decreased during the 1990s, the *Guardian* coherently advanced a strategy of building confidence in science, with an emphasis on consensus as a means of enhancing the reliability of knowledge. This was because the *Guardian* understood and promoted one of the fundamental bases of science, which is that a theory, such as global warming, can only be accepted or rejected by the weight of evidence. So, as evidence from many different areas of science continues to support the theory of global warming, so correspondingly our confidence in the theory should increase. Far from painting science as 'pure' or 'correct', instead the *Guardian* politicized it to demonstrate the bias that is inherent in all science. This clearly showed that many of the climate change claims were being eroded by lobbying pressure, mainly associated with the fossil-fuel industry. This politicizing of science allowed the

*Guardian* to strengthen their readers' confidence in science. Moreover, they clearly conveyed the uncertainties that the science of the global warming hypothesis contains and were and still are in favour of the precautionary principle. It was through this media filter that scientists attempted to advance their particular global warming view, by either making claims for more research or promoting certain political options. From the late 1980s onwards, scientists became very adept at staging their media performances, and it is clear that the general acceptance of the global warming hypothesis is in part due to their continued effort to communicate their findings. Indeed, both the sceptical and the supportive stances of *The Times* and *Guardian*, respectively, so legitimized the debate over global warming that the public became aware that this was not an overnight news story but something that has become part of the very fabric of our society.

It seems that the media has also influenced our use of words. From 1988 onwards the use of the phrase 'global warming' and 'climate change' gained support, while 'greenhouse effect' lost its appeal and by 1997 was rarely mentioned. The change in terminology is reflected in this book. The title is *Global Warming*, as everyone knows what it means, and the major discussions in this book are about the climate change it might induce.

So by combining (1) the science of global warming essentially carried out by the mid-1960s, (2) the frightening upturn in the global temperature data set at the end of the 1980s, (3) our increased knowledge of how past climate has reacted to changes in atmospheric carbon dioxide in the 1980s, (4) the emergence of the global environmental awareness in the late 1980s, and (5) the media's savage interest in the confrontational nature of the debate, we are led to the final recognition of the global warming hypothesis. This has culminated in thousands of scientists turning their attention to the problem to try to prove it right or wrong. Landmarks since then have been the setting up of the Intergovernmental Panel on Climate Change (IPCC) in 1988 by the United Nations Environmental Panel and World Meteorological Organization; the publication of key reports by the IPCC in 1990, 1996, and 2001; the formal signature of the United Nations Framework Convention on Climate Change (UNFCCC) at the Rio Earth Summit in 1992; the subsequent Conference of the Parties (COP) at Kyoto in 1998, where the UNFCCC Protocols were formally accepted, and then in Bonn in July 2001, where the so-called 'Kyoto' Protocols were agreed by 186 countries.

# Chapter 3
# Your viewpoint determines the future

Considering all the scientific evidence collected to support the global warming hypothesis, why is there still a huge range of opinions on what the future holds for us? An interesting way of viewing this problem has been presented by Professor John Adams at University College London. He suggests it is all down to how each individual views risk, in particular how we view 'nature' as a risk. Do we believe that nature is benign and able to take whatever we throw at it or do we think of it as malevolent, having the power to react harshly to our interference? As Douglas and Wildavsky (1983) ask and answer in their book, 'Can we know the risks we face now and in the future? No, we cannot, but yes, we must act as if we do.' We all have to predict what the risks are around us, both at the present time and in the future. This applies to anything from the risk of crossing the road to the risk of climate change from global warming. John Adams has developed 'four myths of nature' and 'four myths of human nature' and combined them to look at the range of individual responses to risk and uncertainty (Adams, 1995). What I have done here is to alter these myths slightly so they are more directly related to the issue of global warming. It must be remembered that these are just another way of appreciating how different people see the global warming hypothesis.

Nature benign

Nature ephemeral

Nature perverse/tolerant

Nature capricious

**8. The four myths of nature**

Adams (1995) suggest there are Four myths of nature which are shown in Figure 8:

1. *Nature benign.* Nature, according to this myth, is predictable, bountiful, robust, stable, and forgiving of any insults that humankind might inflict upon it. However violently it might be shaken, the ball always comes to rest in the bottom of the basin. If nature is benign in the context of human activity then it does not need to be managed and thus a non-interventionist approach can be taken.

2. *Nature ephemeral.* Nature is fragile, precarious, and unforgiving. It is in danger of catastrophic collapse thanks to human interference. The objective of environmental management must therefore be to protect nature from humans. This myth insists that people must tread lightly on the Earth and that the guiding management rule is one of precaution.

3. *Nature perverse/tolerant.* This is a combination of the first two myths. Within limits, nature can be relied upon to behave

predictably. It is forgiving of modest shocks to the system but care must be taken not to knock the ball out of the cup. Regulation is required to prevent major excesses while leaving the system to look after itself in minor matters. This is the ecologist's equivalent of a mixed-economy model. The management style is interventionist.

4. *Nature capricious*. Nature is unpredictable. The appropriate management style is laissez-faire, as there is no point to management. The believer in this myth is an agnostic concerning nature as the future may turn out to be good or bad, but in any event it is beyond any human control.

Individuals base their views on many factors: on their own belief system, their own personal agenda (either financial or political), or whatever is expedient to believe at the time. However, the basis to everyone's views of the global warming hypothesis is determined by how we each perceive the world. Cultural geographers and sociologists have suggested a grid system to look at individual beliefs. One axis on the horizontal from left to right is a measure of how human nature can vary from an individualist to a more collectivist point of view, while the vertical axis varies from the top 'Prescribed Inequality', a measure of the amount of restrictions one feels is imposed by a superior authority, assuming of course that all social and economic transactions are characterized by inequality. At the bottom, 'Prescribing Equality', there are no externally prescribed constraints on choice and people negotiate the rules as they go along. Combining these two axes produces four myths of human nature which can then be combined with our views of nature.

The four myths of human nature associated with this grid are shown in Figure 9.

1. *Individualists* are enterprising 'self-made' people relatively free from control by others, who strive to exert control over their

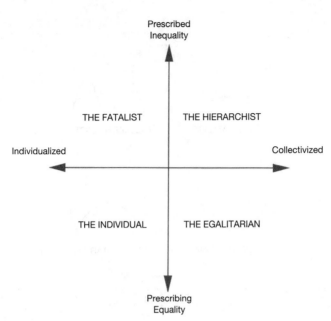

THE FATALIST     THE HIERARCHIST

Individualized           Collectivized

THE INDIVIDUAL    THE EGALITARIAN

Prescribed
Inequality

Prescribing
Equality

9. **Four myths of human nature**

environment and the people in it. Their success is often measured by their wealth and the number of followers they can command. Victorian mill owners or self-made oil barons are good representatives of this category.

2. *Hierarchists,* who inhabit a world with strong group boundaries and binding prescriptions. Social relationships in this world are hierarchical and everyone knows his or her place. Soldiers, civil servants, and certain kinds of scientist are exemplars of this category.

3. *Egalitarians* have strong group loyalties but little respect for externally imposed rules, other than those imposed by nature. Group decisions are arrived at democratically and leaders rule by

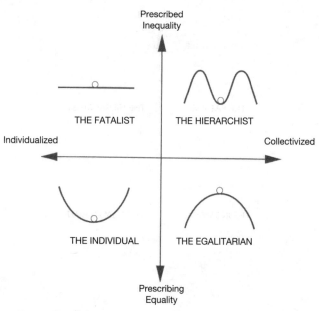

**10. Four rationalities**

force of personality and persuasion. Environmental pressure groups are a classic example of this category.

4. *Fatalists* have minimal control over their own lives. They belong to no groups responsible for decisions that rule their lives. They are resigned to their fate and everyone else's, and see no point in trying to change it.

These two sets of myths can be related to each other to explain what type of person is likely to believe which myth of nature (see Figure 10). What I have done in Figure 11 is to overlay some of the possible climatic changes that could occur as a result of global warming, changes which were discussed in Chapter 1. Now, for fun, you should try putting the following people on the global warming belief chart: yourself, President George Bush, a Greenpeace spokesperson,

40

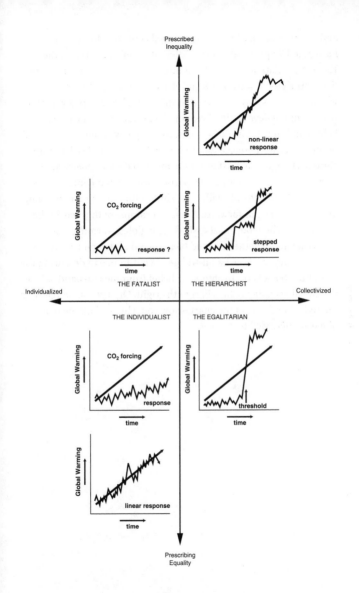

**11. Combined global warming scenarios with myths of human nature**

and a cotton farmer in a less-developed country. Also, when you have read Chapter 8 about the different groups involved in the Kyoto Negotiations, it may be of interest to see where each group lies on the global warming belief chart. By looking at global warming in this way it shows that there are clear reasons why those who do not believe in the threat of global warming may never believe in it until it is too late, because they have their own view of nature and thus perceive that there is a low potential risk of future climate change. We must also remember that individuals can be extremely fluid in their beliefs, particularly when it comes to risk and uncertainty. People will, thus, shift in their opinion depending on the evidence put forward. A classic example of this was in the mid-1990s when journalists asked me if global warming was occurring and whether I would be prepared to defend it; now, by contrast, they ask how bad it will get. What I hope to do during the rest of the book is try to shift your belief from the left-hand side of the global warming belief chart to the right. Or, if you are already on the right-hand side of the chart, show you why your instinctive view of nature may well be correct.

# Chapter 4
# What is the evidence for climate change?

## Past climate change

Climate change in the geological past has been reconstructed using a number of key archives, including marine and lake sediments, ice cores, cave deposits, and tree rings. These various records reveal that over the last 100 million years the Earth's climate has been cooling down, moving from the so-called 'Greenhouse World' of the Cretaceous Period, when dinosaurs enjoyed warm and gentle conditions, through to the cooler and more dynamic 'Ice House World' of today (see Figure 12). It may seem odd that in geological terms our planet is relatively cold, while this whole book is concerned with our great fears of global warming. This is because even today we have huge ice sheets on both Antarctica and Greenland and nearly permanent sea ice in the Arctic Ocean. So, compared to the time of the dinosaurs, when there were no massive ice sheets, we live in chilly times.

This long-term, 100-million-year transition to cooler global climate conditions was driven mainly by tectonic changes, such as the opening of the Tasmanian–Antarctic gateway and the Drake passage, which isolated Antarctica from the rest of the world, the uplift of the Himalayas, and the closure of the Panama ocean gateway. There is also geological evidence that levels of atmospheric carbon dioxide have become significantly lower over the last 100 million years. These changes culminated in the glaciation of

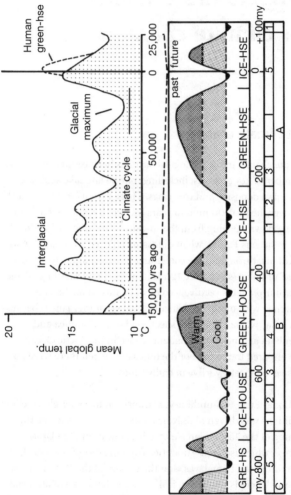

12. **The anatomy of past climatic changes**

Antarctica about 35 million years ago and then the great northern hemisphere ice ages, which began 2.5 million years ago. Since the beginning of the great northern ice ages the global climate has cycled from conditions that were similar or even slightly warmer than today, to full ice ages, which caused ice sheets over 3 km thick to form over much of North America and Europe. Between 2.5 and 0.9 million years ago these glacial-interglacial cycles occurred every 41,000 years and since 0.9 million years ago they have occurred every 100,000 years. These great ice-age cycles are driven primarily by changes in the Earth's orbit with respect to the sun. In fact the world has spent over 80% of the last 2.5 million years in conditions colder than the present. Our present interglacial, the Holocene Period, started about 10,000 years ago and is an example of the rare warm conditions that occur between each ice age. The Holocene began with the rapid and dramatic end of the last ice age; in less than 4,000 years global temperatures increased by 6°C, relative sea level rose by 120 m, atmospheric carbon dioxide increased by a third, and atmospheric methane doubled.

It may seem strange in a book about global warming to suggest that we are currently in a geological 'Ice House World'. This is, however, an important point when we look at the consequences of the world warming up, because, despite being in a relatively warm interglacial period, both poles are still glaciated, which is a rare occurrence in the geological history of our planet. Antarctica and Greenland are covered by ice sheets, and the majority of the Arctic Ocean is covered with sea ice. This means that there is a lot of ice that could melt in a warmer world, and, as we will see, this is one of the biggest unknowns that the future holds for our planet. The two glaciated poles also make the temperature gradient or difference between the poles and the Equator extremely large, from an average of about + 30°C at the Equator down to −35°C or colder at the poles. This temperature gradient is one of the main reasons that we have a climate system, as excess heat from the tropics is exported both via the oceans and the atmosphere to the poles, which causes our weather. Geologically, we currently have one of the largest Equator–

pole temperature gradients, which leads to a very dynamic climate system. So our 'Ice House' conditions cause our very energetic weather system, which is characterized by hurricanes, tornadoes, extra-tropical (temperate) winter storms, and monsoons. James Lovelock in his book 'The Ages of Gaia' (New edition, 1995 p. 227) suggests that interglacials, like the Holocene Period, are the fevered state of our planet, which clearly over the last 2.5 million years prefers a colder average global temperature. Lovelock sees global warming as humanity just adding to the fever.

Climate, however, has not been constant during our interglacial, i.e. the last 10,000 years. Palaeoclimate evidence suggests that the early Holocene was warmer than the 20th century. Throughout the Holocene there have been millennial-scale climate events, called Dansgaard-Oeschger cycles, which involve a local cooling of 2°C. These events have had a significant influence on classical civilizations; for example, the cold arid event about 4,000 years ago coincides with the collapse of many classical civilizations, such as the Old Kingdom in Egypt (see discussion in Chapter 9). The last of these millennial climate cycles was the Little Ice Age. This event is really two cold periods; the first follows the Medieval Warm Period which ended a thousand years ago, and is often referred to as the Medieval Cold Period. The Medieval Cold Period played a role in extinguishing Norse colonies on Greenland and caused famine and mass migration in Europe. It started gradually before AD 1200 and ended at about AD 1650. The second cold period, more classically referred to as the Little Ice Age, may have been the most rapid and largest change in the North Atlantic region during the late Holocene, as suggested by ice-core and deep-sea sediment records. The reconstruction of temperature records for the last thousand years includes the Little Ice Age and is essential data for demonstrating that the last two centuries are very different from the preceding eight (Figure 13). There are four main data sets which have attempted to reconstruct temperatures for the northern hemisphere over the last millennium: tree rings, corals, ice cores, and/or the direct measurement of past temperatures from

46

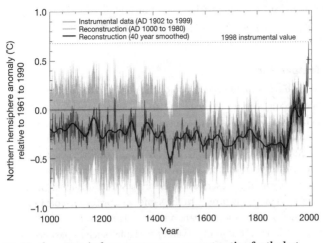

**13. Northern Hemisphere temperature reconstruction for the last thousand years**

boreholes. First, it should be noted that the different data sets compare well with each other, which gives added confidence that we are seeing real temperature variations in these reconstructions. Second, the data show that the centuries before 1900 were much colder. They also show that the Medieval Warm Period and the Little Ice Age did occur, but that in much of the northern hemisphere the climate changes seen are only small, with the exception of northern Europe. Without this data the instrumental temperature data set for the last 150 years would have no context. As it is, it can now be clearly shown that temperatures, at least for the northern hemisphere, have been warmer in the 20th century than at any other time during the last thousand years.

## Recent climate change

The three main indicators of global warming are temperature, precipitation, and sea level. One of the key aims of scientists over the last couple of decades has been to estimate how these have changed since the industrial revolution and to see if there is any evidence for global warming being to blame. Below is the evidence for each of these parameters.

## Temperature

As we have seen, temperatures for the northern hemisphere have been reconstructed for the last thousand years, providing a context to the 20th century. Temperatures for the last 150 years have been estimated from a number of sources, both direct thermometer-based indicators and proxy-based. What is a proxy? As used here and elsewhere, it is short for proxy variable. The term 'proxy' is commonly used to describe a stand-in or substitute, as in 'proxy vote' or 'fighting by proxy'. In the same way, proxy variable in the parlance of climatology means a measurable 'descriptor' that stands in for a desired (but unobservable) 'variable', such as past ocean or land temperature. So there is an assumption that you can use the proxy variable to estimate a climatic variable that you cannot measure directly. So, as we will see below, you can use the thickness of tree rings as a way of estimating past land temperatures; in this case, the tree-ring thickness is a proxy for temperature.

Thermometer-based indicators include sea-surface temperature (SST), marine air temperatures (MAT), land surface-air temperature, and temperatures in the free atmosphere, such as those measured by sensors on balloons. Borehole temperature measurements are defined as proxy-based because, despite the use of direct measurements of temperatures, these have been altered over time. Mathematical inversion procedures are required to translate the modern temperature in the boreholes into changes of ground temperature back through time. Other proxy-based methods include infrared satellite measurements and tree-ring width and thickness.

Thermometer-based measurements of air temperature have been recorded at a number of sites in North America and Europe as far back as 1760. The number of observation sites does not increase to sufficient worldwide geographical coverage to permit a global land average to be calculated until about the middle of the 19th century. SST and marine air temperatures were systematically recorded by ships from the mid-19th century, but even today the coverage of the southern hemisphere is extremely poor. All these data sets require various corrections to account for changing conditions and measurement techniques. For example, for land data each station has been examined to ensure that conditions have not varied through time as a result of changes in the measurement site, instruments used, instrument shelters, or the way monthly averages were computed, or the growth of cities around the sites, which leads to warmer temperatures caused by the urban heat island effect.

For SST and MAT there are a number of corrections that have to be applied. First, up to 1941 most SST temperature measurements were made in sea water hoisted on deck in a bucket. Since 1941 most measurements have been made at the ships' engine water intakes. Second, between 1856 and 1910 there was a shift from wooden to canvas buckets, which changes the amount of cooling caused by evaporation that occurs as the water is being hoisted on deck. In addition, through this period there was a gradual shift from sailing ships to steamships, which altered the height of the ship decks and the speed of the ships, both of which can affect the evaporative cooling of the buckets. The other key correction that has to be made is for the global distribution of meteorological stations through time. As shown in Figure 14, the number of stations and their location varies greatly from 1870 to 1960. But by making these corrections it is possible to produce a continuous record of land-surface air and SST temperature for the last 130 years, which shows a global warming of 0.65°C ±0.05°C over this period.

What is so interesting about the 130-year temperature data set are the details, particularly as mentioned before the cooling observed in the 1960s and 1970s. One of the key tests for climate models, used to predict future climate changes, is whether they can reproduce the changes seen since 1870. These models are discussed in more detail

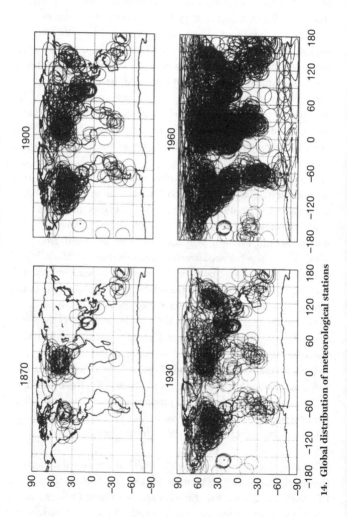

**14. Global distribution of meteorological stations**

in the next chapter but it should be noted that only by combining natural forcing (such as solar 11-year cycles and stratospheric aerosols from explosive volcanic eruptions), and anthropogenic forcing (greenhouse gases and sulphur aerosols) can the temperature record be simulated.

For the last 40 years balloon data has been available. In 1958 an initial network of 540 stations was set up to release rawindsondes, or balloons, which were regularly released to measure temperature, relative humidity, and pressure through the atmosphere to a height of about 20 km, where they burst. By the 1970s the network had grown to 700–800 stations reporting twice daily. The balloon data set shows a general surface and lower troposphere warming over the last 30 years of about 0.1–0.2 °C/10 years, while weak cooling is seen in the upper troposphere and strong cooling in the stratosphere.

Satellite-based proxy records have been available for the last 20 years and have been the source of some key controversies in the global warming debate. The advantage of satellite-mounted microwave sensors is that they have a global coverage, unlike the balloons which are predominately land-based and in the northern hemisphere. There are, however, some major problems with the microwave data set. First, the temperature record is based on eight different satellites, and despite overlapping measurement times, intercalibration between different instruments is problematic. Second, there is a spurious warming trend after 1990 of 0.03–0.04 °C which is due to a drift in the orbital times, and a spurious cooling trend of 0.12°C/decade due to the reduced altitude or height of the satellites caused by friction with the atmosphere. Third, the height within the atmosphere at which the microwave sensor measures temperature is affected by the amount of ice crystals and raindrops in the atmosphere. Hence, if the planet is warming up, moisture will be found at great altitude, and the microwave sensor would in fact measure temperature much higher in the atmosphere, i.e. in the colder parts of the troposphere, thus giving a smaller temperature increase than that which actually occurred. It is unsurprising that reports on satellite recorded global temperature trends for the last 30 years have changed, as every new paper published contains yet another correction that must be considered. For example, huge controversy occurred when Christy *et al.* (1995) deduced a global mean cooling trend of 0.05°C/decade for the period 1979–94, but obtained a warming trend of 0.09°C/decade over this period by removing the effects of El Niño and the climatic effect of the eruption of Mount Pinatubo. When the data set is corrected for decreasing satellite altitude, the global mean cooling turns into a warming of 0.07°C/decade. If the balloon, surface, and satellite data are compared, there is some agreement and it shows that the surface and lower troposphere have been warming up, while the stratosphere has been cooling down. An excellent summary of the corrections that have been made to each data set and why they were applied can be found in Harvey (2000).

The Intergovernmental Panel on Climate Change (IPCC) has collated all the published land-surface air and sea-surface temperatures from 1861 to 1998, with all the corrections discussed above. This data is shown relative to the average temperature between 1961 and 1990 in Figure 13, and, as you can see, there has been a sharp warming from the start of the 1980s onwards. The mean global surface temperature has increased by about 0.3 to 0.6°C since the late 19th century. Including the evidence from balloons and satellites, there seems to be a 0.2 to 0.3°C increase over the last 40 years, which is the period with most reliable data. Recent years have been among the warmest since 1860 – the period for which instrumental records are available. This warming is evident in both sea-surface and land-based surface air temperatures. Indirect indicators, such as borehole temperatures and glacier shrinkage, provide independent support for the observed warming. It should also be noted that the warming has not been globally uniform. The recent warming has been greatest between 40°N and 70°N latitude, though some areas such as the North Atlantic Ocean have cooled in the recent decades.

## Precipitation

There are two global precipitation data sets: 'Hulme' and the 'Global Historical Climate Network' (GHCN). Unfortunately, unlike temperature, rainfall and snow records are not as well documented and the records have not been carried out for as long. It is also known that precipitation over land tends to be underestimated by up to 10–15% owing to the effects of airflow around the collecting dish. The gradual realization and correction of this effect has produced a spurious upward trend in global precipitation. After correction, there is an overall increase of precipitation of 1% over land, which is so small that it cannot be distinguished from zero, i.e. no change. A detailed view suggests that, taking an average over the Earth's land surface, precipitation increased from the start of the century up to about 1960, but has decreased since about 1980. But yet again, as with main key data sets concerning global warming, we have a huge gap, which is due to the lack of data on precipitation over the oceans. However, what is observed are some significant changes in where the precipitation has occurred (Figure 15). It seems that precipitation has increased over land at high latitudes in the northern hemisphere, especially during the cold season. One study also suggested that there was an increase in the amount of rain falling during heavy rain events, especially in the USA, the former Soviet Union, and China. Decreases in precipitation occurred after the 1960s over the subtropics and the tropics from Africa to Indonesia. These changes are consistent with available data analyses of changes in stream flow, lake levels, and soil surface. In terms of snowfall, Antarctic is a big winner with an increase of 5–20% over the last two decades, while Greenland has lost about 20% of its snow accumulation over the last 50 years.

## Relative sea level

The IPCC has also put together a key data set of sea level. In general it shows that over the last 100 years, the global sea level has risen by about 4 to 14 cm (Figure 16). But sea-level change is difficult to measure, as relative sea-level changes have been derived mainly from tide-gauge data. In the conventional tide-gauge system, the

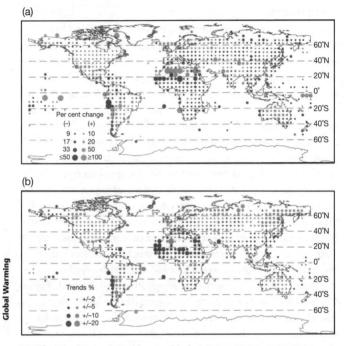

(a)

(b)

**15. Changes in precipitation over land a) 1955–1974 to 1975–1994 and b) 1900 to 1994**

sea level is measured relative to a land-based tide-gauge benchmark. The major problem is that the land surface is much more dynamic that one would expect, with a lot of vertical movements, and these get incorporated into the measurements. Vertical movements can occur as a result of normal geological compaction of delta sediments, the withdrawal of groundwater from coastal aquifers (both of which are discussed in more detail in Chapter 6, Coastline section), uplift associated with colliding tectonic plates (the most extreme of which is mountain building such as the Himalayas), or ongoing postglacial rebound and compensation elsewhere associated with the end of the last ice age. The latter is caused by the rapid removal of weight when the giant ice sheets melted, so that the land which has been weighed down slowly rebounds back to its original position. An example of this is Scotland, which is rising at a rate of 3 mm/year while England is still sinking at a rate of 2 mm/year, despite the Scottish ice sheet having melted 10,000 years ago. Again, using a number of corrections, the global tide-gauge network suggests that the rise in sea level since the beginning of the 20th century could be as much as 18 cm (~1.8±0.1 mm/year). On this timescale, the warming and the consequent thermal expansion of the oceans may account for about 2–7 cm of the observed sea-level rise, while the observed retreat of glaciers may account for about 2–5 cm. Other factors are more difficult to quantify. The rate of observed sea-level rise suggests that there may have been a net positive contribution from the huge ice sheets of Greenland and Antarctica, but observations of these ice sheets suggest that there may have been a net expansion which would have contributed –0.05 mm/year to global sea level over the last 100 years. The ice sheets remain a major source of uncertainty in accounting for past changes in sea level because of insufficient data about these ice sheets over the last 100 years.

One of the biggest unknowns of global warming is whether the massive ice sheets over Greenland and Antarctica will melt. A key indicator of the expansion or contraction of these ice sheets is the sea ice that surrounds them. The state of the cryosphere (or the global ice) is extremely important, as shrinking of ice on land causes the sea level to rise. Unfortunately, submarines have already recorded a worrying thinning of the polar ice caps. Sea-ice draft is the thickness of the part of the ice that is submerged under the sea. Therefore, in order to understand the effects of global warming on the cryosphere it is important to measure how much ice is melting in the polar regions. Comparison of sea-ice draft data acquired on submarine cruises between 1993 and 1997 with similar data acquired between 1958 and 1976 indicates that the mean ice draft at the end of the melt season has decreased by about 1.3 m in most of the deep-water portions of the Arctic Ocean, from 3.1 m in 1958–76 to 1.8 m in the 1990s. In summary, ice draft in the 1990s is over a

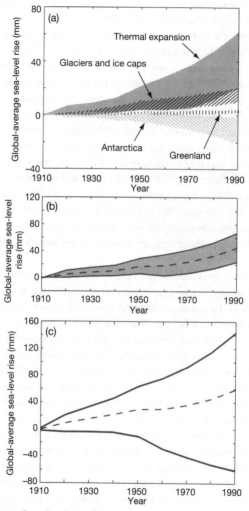

**16. Estimated sea-level rise 1910–1990**

metre thinner than two to four decades earlier. The main draft has decreased from over 3 metres to less than 2 metres and the volume is down by some 40%. In addition, in 2000, for the first time in recorded history, a hole large enough to be seen from space opened in the sea ice above the North Pole. Unfortunately, because satellite records are so short, we do not know if this is a frequent natural occurrence or indicative of significant melting of Arctic sea ice. Moreover, measurements of the size of Greenland suggest that it is shrinking, particularly at its coastal margins.

## Other evidence for global warming

Other evidence for global warming comes from permafrost regions and weather patterns such as particular storm records. In the high latitude and high altitude areas permafrost exists, where it is so cold that the ground is frozen solid to a great depth. During the summer months only the top metre or so of the permafrost gets warm enough to melt, and this is called the active layer. Already in Alaska there seems to have been a 3°C warming down to at least a metre over the last 50 years, showing that the active layer has become deeper. With the massive increases in atmospheric $CO_2$ predicted for the future, it is likely that there will be increases in the thickness of the active layer of the permafrost or perhaps, in some areas, the complete disappearance of so-called discontinuous permafrost over the next century. This widespread loss of permafrost will produce a huge range of problems in local areas, as it will trigger erosion or subsidence, change hydrologic processes, and release into the atmosphere even more $CO_2$ and methane trapped as organic matter in the frozen layers. Hence changes in permafrost will reduce the stability of slopes and thus increase incidence of slides and avalanches. A more dynamic cryosphere will increase the natural hazards for people, structures, and communication links. Already buildings, roads, pipelines, such as the oil pipelines in Alaska, and communication links are being threatened.

There is evidence too that our weather patterns are changing. For example, in recent years massive storms and subsequent floods have hit China, Italy, England, Korea, Bangladesh, Venezuela, and Mozambique. In England in 2000, floods classified as 'once in 30-year events' occurred twice in the same month. Moreover, the winter of 2000/1 was the wettest six months recorded in Britain since records began in the 18th century, while in the summer of 2003 Britain recorded the first ever temperature of 100°F since records began. In addition, on average, British birds nest 12±4 days earlier than 30 years ago. Insect species – including bees and termites – that need warm weather to survive are moving northward, and some have already reached England by crossing the Channel from France. Glaciers in Europe are in retreat, particularly in the Alps and Iceland. Ice cover records from the Tornio River in Finland, which has been recorded since 1693, show that the spring thaw of the frozen river now occurs a month earlier.

There is also evidence that more storms are occurring in the northern hemisphere. Wave height in the North Atlantic Ocean has been monitored since the early 1950s, from lightships, Ocean Weather Stations, and more recently satellites. Between the 1950s and 1990s the average wave height increased from 2.5 to 3.5 m, an increase of 40%. Storm intensity is the major control over wave height, which provides evidence for an increase in storm activity over the last 40 years. This is supported by German scientists who suggested that storm-generated ocean waves pounding the coasts of Europe produce long-wave vibrations which are picked up by the sensitive equipment set up to record earthquakes. From this evidence they calculated the number of storm days per month during the winter. It seems that over the last 50 years these have increased from seven to 14 days per month. This also fits with the observed increase in winter extratropical cyclones, i.e. those occurring in the mid-latitudes, which have increased markedly over the last hundred years, with significant increases in both the Pacific and Atlantic sectors since the early 1970s. There has, however, in contrast, been a slight downturn in the number of hurricanes over the last 50 years.

17. Mozambique floods of 2000

## What do the sceptics say?

One of the best ways to summarize the evidence for global warming and to persuade you, the reader, that there is evidence that humanity has already altered global climate, is to review what the sceptics say against the global warming hypothesis:

1. Ice-core data suggest atmospheric $CO_2$ responds to global temperature, therefore, atmospheric $CO_2$ cannot cause global temperature changes.

A detailed examination of the ice-core $CO_2$ data at the end of the last glacial period shows that the major stepwise increases occur at the same time as warming in Antarctica. It is known that during the last de-glaciation, gradual warming in Antarctica occurred before step-like warming in the northern hemisphere (Figure 18). There is, therefore, excellent evidence that atmospheric carbon dioxide increases before overall global temperatures rise and the ice sheets begin to melt. In fact, there is clear evidence that Antarctic temperatures and atmospheric carbon dioxide levels are in step (Figure 18), demonstrating the central role of carbon dioxide as a climate amplifier. Moreover, time-series analysis of the last four glacial-interglacial cycles by Professor Shackleton at Cambridge University suggests atmospheric carbon dioxide response up to 5,000 years before variations in global ice sheets. This has prompted many palaeoclimatologists to re-evaluate the role of atmospheric carbon dioxide, placing it now as a primary driving force of past climate instead of a secondary response and feedback.

2. Every data set showing global warming has been corrected or tweaked to achieve this desired result.

For people who are not regularly involved in science this seems to be the biggest problem with the whole 'global warming has happened' argument. As I have shown, all the data sets covering the last 150 years require some sort of adjustment. This, though, is part of the

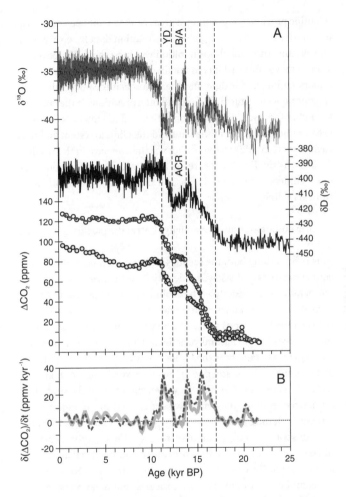

18. Ice core records showing CO₂ in phase with Antarctic warming.
A) $\delta^{18}O$ and $\delta D$ = temperature records, $\Delta CO_2$ changing atmospheric
carbon dioxide levels, higher curve taking into account coral reef and
land vegetation changes since the last ice age. B) rate of change of
carbon dioxide most of which occurs in three large pulses

scientific process. For example, if great care had not been taken over the spurious trends in the global precipitation data base we would now assume that global precipitation was increasing. Moreover, as science moves forward incrementally, it gains more and more understanding and insight into the data sets it is constructing. This constant questioning of all data and interpretations is the core strength of science: each new correction or adjustment is due to a greater understanding of the data and the climate system and thus each new study adds to the confidence that we have in the results. This is why the IPCC report refers to the 'weight of the evidence', as our confidence in science increases if similar results are obtained from very different sources.

3. Solar output and sunspot activity control the past temperatures.

This is something both the sceptics and non-sceptics agree on. Of course sunspots and also volcanic activity influence past temperatures. For example, the cooling of the 1960s and 1970s is clearly linked to changes in the sunspot cycle. The difference between the two camps is that the sceptics put more weight on the importance of these natural variations. Though great care has been taken to understand how the minor variations in solar output affect global climate, this is still one of the areas which contain many unknowns and uncertainties. However, climate models combining our current state-of-the-art knowledge concerning all radiative forcing, including greenhouse gases (see Table 1 on pages 16 and 17) and sunspots, are able to simulate the global temperature curve for the last 130 years. Figure 19 shows the separate natural and anthropogenic forcing on global climate for the last 130 years and the combination of the two. This provides confidence in both models and also an understanding of the relative influence of natural versus anthropogenic forcing.

4. Satellite data casts doubt on the models.

Again, before the satellite data was clearly understood it did suggest

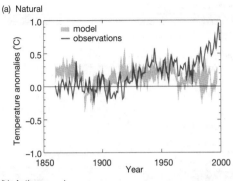

(a) Natural

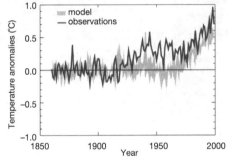

(b) Anthropogenic

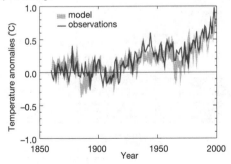

(c) All forcings

19. Simulated annual global mean surface temperatures compared to observed temperatures

(a) Temperature indicators

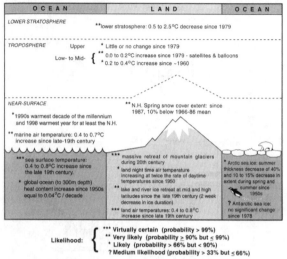

| OCEAN | LAND | OCEAN |
|---|---|---|

*LOWER STRATOSPHERE*

**lower stratosphere: 0.5 to 2.5°C decrease since 1979

*TROPOSPHERE* Upper { * Little or no change since 1979

Low- to Mid- { ** 0.0 to 0.2°C increase since 1979 – satellites & balloons
* 0.2 to 0.4°C increase since ~1960

*NEAR-SURFACE*

** N.H. Spring snow cover extent: since 1987, 10% below 1966-86 mean

* 1990s warmest decade of the millennium and 1998 warmest year for at least the N.H.

** marine air temperature: 0.4 to 0.7°C increase since late-19th century

*** sea surface temperature: 0.4 to 0.8°C increase since the late 19th century.

* global ocean (to 300m depth) heat content increase since 1950s equal to 0.04°C / decade

*** massive retreat of mountain glaciers during 20th century

* land night time air temperature increasing at twice the rate of daytime temperatures since 1950

** lake and river ice retreat at mid and high latitudes since the late 19th century (2 week decrease in ice duration)

*** land air temperatures: 0.4 to 0.8°C increase since late 19th century

* Arctic sea ice: summer thickness decrease of 40% and 10 to 15% decrease in extent during spring and summer since 1950s

? Antarctic sea ice: no significant change since 1978

Likelihood: 
*** **Virtually certain** (probability > 99%)
** **Very likely** (probability ≥ 90% but ≤ 99%)
* **Likely** (probability > 66% but < 90%)
? **Medium likelihood** (probability > 33% but ≤ 66%)

(b) Hydrological and storm-related indicators

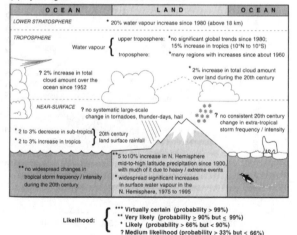

| OCEAN | LAND | OCEAN |
|---|---|---|

*LOWER STRATOSPHERE*

* 20% water vapour increase since 1980 (above 18 km)

*TROPOSPHERE* Water vapour { upper troposphere: *no significant global trends since 1980; 15% increase in tropics (10°N to 10°S)

troposphere: *many regions with increases since about 1960

? 2% increase in total cloud amount over the ocean since 1952

* 2% increase in total cloud amount over land during the 20th century

*NEAR-SURFACE*

? no systematic large-scale change in tornadoes, thunder-days, hail

? no consistent 20th century change in extra-tropical storm frequency / intensity

* 2 to 3% decrease in sub-tropics
* 2 to 3% increase in tropics } 20th century land surface rainfall

** no widespread changes in tropical storm frequency / intensity during the 20th century

** 5 to 10% increase in N. Hemisphere mid-to-high latitude precipitation since 1900, with much of it due to heavy / extreme events

* widespread significant increases in surface water vapour in the N. Hemisphere, 1975 to 1995

Likelihood: 
*** **Virtually certain** (probability > 99%)
** **Very likely** (probability ≥ 90% but ≤ 99%)
* **Likely** (probability > 66% but < 90%)
? **Medium likelihood** (probability > 33% but ≤ 66%)

**20. Schematic of observed variations of the temperature indicators and hydrological and storm-related indicators**

that over the last 20 years there had been a slight cooling. The iterative process of science, i.e. the re-examination of data and the assumption concerning the data, clearly showed that there were some major inconsistencies within the satellite data; first, as a result of trying to compare the data from different instruments on different satellites and, second, because of the need to adjust the altitude of the satellite as its orbit shrinks as a result of friction with the atmosphere. The final problem with the satellite data is that 20 years is just too short a time period to find a temperature trend with any confidence. This is because climatic cycles or events will have a major influence on the record and will not be averaged out; for example, the sunspot cycle is 11 years, El Niño–Southern Oscillation is 3–7 years, and the North Atlantic Oscillation is ten years. So which of these cycles is picked up by the 20-year satellite data will strongly influence the direction of the temperature trend.

Figure 20 summarizes the current state of knowledge concerning the climatic changes that have occurred over the last 100 years both in temperatures and the hydrological cycle, while Figure 21 shows the geographic locations where evidence of global warming over the last 100 years has been found. One of the key arguments for me that significant warming and other climatic changes have occurred over the last 100 years is the weight of evidence from so many diverse data sets. When the last 100 years are compared with the last 1,000 years it is very clear that something completely different is occurring. The evidence suggests that natural climate forcings such as sunspots and volcanic eruptions have been similar for the last millennium. This leaves only one alternative – that greenhouses gases, with their known radiative forcing, have already influenced global climate. From the huge amount of published scientific evidence the IPCC (2001) has concluded: 'In the light of new evidence and taking into account the remaining uncertainties, most of the observed warming over the last 50 years is likely [60–90% confidence] to be due to the increase in greenhouse gas concentration.'

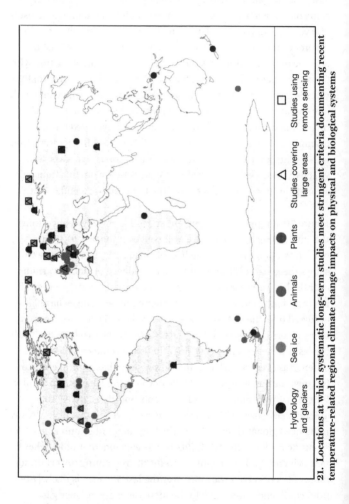

21. Locations at which systematic long-term studies meet stringent criteria documenting recent temperature-related regional climate change impacts on physical and biological systems

# Chapter 5
# How do you model the future?

You may not believe this, but the whole of human society operates on knowing the future, particularly the weather. For example, a farmer in India knows when the monsoon rains will come next year and so when to plant his crops, while a farmer in Indonesia knows there are two monsoon rains next year so he can plant crops twice. This is based on their knowledge of the past as the monsoons have always come at about the same time each year in living memory. But such a prediction goes deeper than this as it influences every part of our lives. Our houses are built for the local climate – in England that means central heating but no air conditioning, while in the southern USA it is vice versa. Road, railways, airports, offices, cars, trains, etc. are all designed for the local climate. This is why in the spring of 2003 a centimetre of snow one afternoon effectively shut down London, while Toronto can easily deal with and function with half a metre of snow. In England in 2003 people were complaining about the heat when the temperature touched 100°F for the first time in recorded history, which colleagues of mine both in the USA and Africa found extremely amusing, while Australians go into shock if the temperature drops below 50°F. The problem with global warming is that it changes the rules. The past weather of an area cannot be relied on to tell you what the future will hold. So we have to develop new ways of predicting the future, so that we can plan our lives and so that human society can continue to fully function. So the very simple answer to the chapter title is that we *have* to model the future.

There is a whole hierarchy of climate models from relatively simple box models to the extremely complex three-dimensional general circulation models (GCMs). Each has a role in examining and furthering our understanding of the global climate system. However, it is the complex three-dimensional general circulation models which are used to predict future global climate. These comprehensive climate models are based on physical laws represented by mathematical equations that are solved using a three-dimensional grid over the globe. To obtain the most realistic simulations, all the major parts of the climate system must be represented in sub-models, including atmosphere, ocean, land surface (topography), cryosphere, and biosphere, as well as the processes that go on within them and between them. Most global climate models have at least some representation of each of these components. Models that couple together both the ocean and atmosphere components are called Atmosphere-Ocean General Circulation Models (AOGCMs). The development of climate models over the last two decades is shown in Figure 22. Models of different parts of the climate system are first developed separately and then coupled into the comprehensive climate models. For example, the Met Office Hadley Centre model is the first AOGCM which now has a fully coupled 'dynamic vegetation' model. This is important because it has long been known that vegetation has an influence on climate; thus climate changes can affect the vegetation and those changes in vegetation can have an effect on climate. For example, the Amazon rainforest recycles about half the precipitation that falls, maintaining a moist continental interior which would otherwise be dry.

One of the key aspects of climate models is the detail in which they can reconstruct the world; this is usually termed spatial resolution. In general the current generation of AOGCMs have a resolution or detail of the atmosphere of one point every 250 km

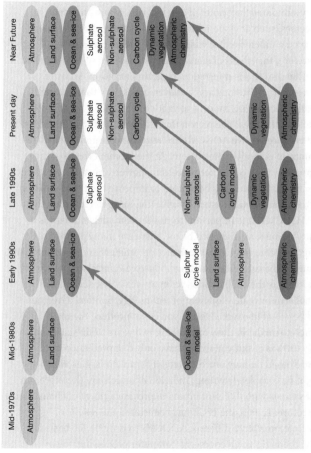

22. The development of climate models, past, present, and future

by 250 km in the horizontal and about 1 km in the vertical above the boundary layer. This would mean the atmosphere above the British Isles was represented by only ten points. The resolution of a typical ocean model is about 200–400 m in the vertical and 125–250 km in the horizontal. Equations are typically solved for every simulated 'half hour' of a model run. Many physical processes, such as cloud and ocean convection, of course take place on a much smaller scale than the model can resolve. Therefore, the effects of small-scale processes have to be lumped together and this is referred to as parametrization. Many of these parametrizations are, however, checked with separate 'small-scale-process models' to validate the scaling up of these smaller influences. The reason that the spatial scale is limited is that comprehensive AOGCMs are very complex and use a huge amount of computer time to run. At the moment much of the improvement in computer processing power which has occurred over the last decade has been used to improve the representation of the global climate system by coupling more models directly to the AOGCMs. It is important to run these models numerous times because, as discussed below, there are many parts of the climate system for which the future parameters are uncertain. For example, the future human greenhouse gas emissions, which are not fixed, as they will depend on many variables, such as the global economy, development of technology, political agreements, and personal lifestyles. Hence, you could produce the most complete model in the world taking two years to simulate the next 100 years, but you would have only one prediction of the future based on only one estimate of future emissions which might be completely wrong. Individual models are therefore run many times with different inputs to provide a range of changes in the future. In fact, the IPCC have consulted the results of multiple runs of 22 different AOGCMs to provide the basis for their predictions. Of course, as computer processing power continues to increase, both this representation of coupled climate systems and the spatial scale will continue to improve. So what are the unknowns and why do we need to run many different model scenarios? Is there not just one view of the future? Unfortunately not, and below each of the unknowns is described in more detail and how it effects our model predictions for the future.

## Carbon cycle

One of the fundamental considerations for the AOGCMs is not whether carbon dioxide influences global temperatures, but rather the extent to which it influences global temperatures. This is not only because of the direct effect of the carbon dioxide but also because of the many secondary influences and other climate feedbacks, such as aerosols, ocean circulation, etc., which may even cool the climate system. The first problem is estimating how much of the anthropogenic carbon dioxide makes it into the atmosphere. You will be surprised to know that about half of all our carbon emissions are absorbed by the natural carbon cycle and do not end up in the atmosphere, but rather in the oceans and the terrestrial biosphere. This leads us to realize that we need to understand the present-day carbon cycle in order to understand the amount of carbon dioxide that will end up in the atmosphere.

The Earth's carbon cycle is extremely complicated, with both sources and sinks of carbon dioxide. Figure 23 shows the global carbon reservoirs in GtC (gigatonnes, or 1,000 million tonnes) and fluxes (the ins and outs of carbon in GtC per year). These indicated figures are annual averages over the period 1980–9. It must be remembered that the component cycles have been simplified, and the figures only present average values. The amount of carbon stored and transported by rivers, particularly the anthropogenic portion, is currently very poorly quantified and is not shown here. Evidence is accumulating that many of the fluxes can vary significantly from year to year. In contrast to the static view conveyed in figures like this one, the carbon system is dynamic, and coupled to the climate system on seasonal, inter-annual, and

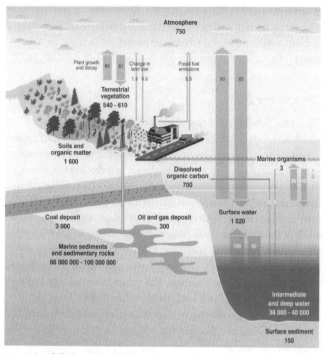

**23. A simplified version of the present carbon cycle**

decadal timescales. The most interesting figure is that the surface ocean takes up just less than half the carbon dioxide produced by industry per year. However, this is one of the most poorly known figures and there is still considerable debate over whether the oceans will continue to be such a large sink or absorber of our pollution. As we will see in Chapter 7, one of the great surprises recently has been the unexpected experimental results which suggest that the Amazon rainforest could be absorbing large quantities of atmospheric carbon dioxide. The key question we need to ask, if indeed this is the case, is: for how long will the oceans and the Amazon rainforest continue to absorb carbon dioxide?

# Cooling effects

As well as the warming effects of the greenhouse gases, the Earth's climate system is complicated in that that there are also cooling effects (see Figure 24 for the IPCC summary of both warming and cooling effects). This includes the amount of particles in the air (which are technically called aerosols, many of which come from human pollution such as sulphur emissions from power stations) and these have a direct effect on the amount of solar radiation that hits the Earth's surface. Aerosols may have significant local or regional impact on temperature. In fact, the AOGCMs have now factored them into the computer simulations of global warming, and they provide an explanation of why industrial areas of the planet have not warmed as much as previously predicted. Water vapour is a greenhouse gas, but, at the same time, the upper white surface of clouds reflects solar radiation back into space. This reflection is called albedo – and clouds and ice have a high albedo and so reflect large quantities of solar radiation from surfaces on Earth. Predicting what will happen to the amount and types of clouds, and the extent of global ice in the future, creates huge difficulties in calculating the exact effect of global warming. For example, if the polar ice cap melts, the albedo will be significantly reduced, as this ice would be replaced by vegetation or open water, both of which absorb heat rather than reflecting it like white snow or ice. This would produce a positive feedback, enhancing the effects of global warming.

# Economic models of the future

A critical problem with trying to predict future climate is predicting the amount of carbon dioxide emissions that will be produced in the future. This will be influenced by population growth, economic growth, Third World development, fossil-fuel usage, the rate at which we switch to alternative energy, the rate of deforestation, and whether an international agreement to cut emissions is ever

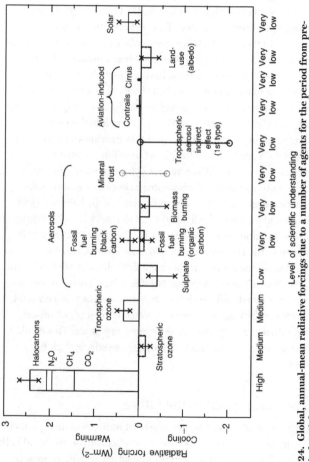

24. Global, annual-mean radiative forcings due to a number of agents for the period from pre-industrial to present

reached. Out of all the systems that we are trying to model into the future, humanity is by far the most complicated and unpredictable. If you want to understand the problem of predicting what will happen in the next hundred years image yourself in 1904 and what you would have predicted the world to be like in 2004. Would you have predicted the explosion of car use or the general availability of flight? Even ten years ago it would have been difficult to predict the budget airlines which allow for such cheap flights throughout Europe and the USA.

So what the IPCC has done is to produce 40 new scenarios of what the future could be like depending on the factors above. Of these there are worst-cases scenarios, which predict an increase of 220% in atmospheric carbon dioxide by 2100, compared with pre-industrial levels, and best-case scenarios which still predict a 75% increase by 2100 (Figure 25a). Even if the anthropogenic emissions of carbon dioxide are stabilized or even reduced, the carbon dioxide content in the atmosphere is still expected to increase over the next 100 years. Because of these different economic models or visions of the future, the IPCC has switched from trying to predict the future to discussing projections and possible futures. Bjørn Lomborg provides an interesting and radical insight to the IPCC's 40 future scenarios in his controversial book *The Skeptical Environmentalist* (2001).

## Future global temperatures and sea level

Seven AOGCMs have been run using selected future carbon dioxide emission scenarios for the IPCC 2001 report to produce global average temperature changes that may occur by 2100. These climate models show that the global mean surface temperature could rise by between 1.4°C and 5.8°C by 2100 (see Figure 25). The topmost curve assumes constant aerosol concentrations beyond 1990, high climate sensitivity, and a significant increase in the emissions of carbon dioxide, and produces an increase of 5.8°C by 2100. The lowest curve assumes constant aerosol concentrations

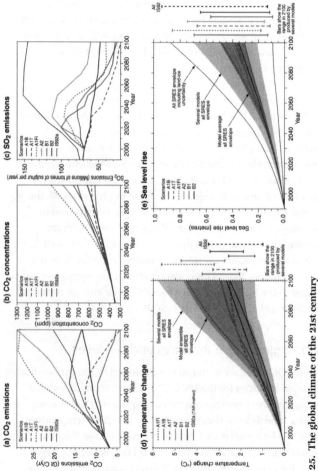

25. **The global climate of the 21st century**

beyond 1990, but a much lower climate sensitivity, and a slower increase in carbon dioxide emissions, and produces an increase of 1.4°C. What is most worrying is that there is a 4.4°C temperature difference between the IPCC projections in the most extreme estimates. However, it should be noted that all the model predictions show an increase in global temperatures over the next hundred years.

Again, using the different carbon dioxide emission scenarios, the IPCC has projected global mean sea level up to 2100. Taking into account the ranges in the estimate of climate sensitivity and ice-melt parameters, and the emission scenarios, the models project an increase in global mean sea level of between 20 cm and 88 cm (Figure 25). Note that during the first half of the 21st century, the choice of emission scenario has relatively little effect on the projected sea-level rise, as most of it is due to the large thermal inertia (i.e. it takes a lot of initial energy to get any noticeable change in temperature) of the ocean–ice–atmosphere climate system. However, it has an increasingly large effect in the latter part of this century, because of the uncertainty about how the ice sheets will react and melt. In addition, because of the thermal inertia of the oceans, sea level would continue to rise for many centuries beyond 2100, even if concentrations of greenhouse gases were stabilized at that time. What the sea-level calculation does not take into account is the possible melting of the world's ice sheets and glaciers. If the ice sheets *completely* melted, their contribution to sea-level rise would be as follows: mountain glaciers = 0.3 m, West Antarctic Ice Sheet = 8.5 m, Greenland = 7 m, East Antarctic Ice Sheet = 65 m. What is worrying is that NASA satellite measurements suggest that both Greenland and the West Antarctic Ice Sheets are shrinking. If this produces enough melt-water then we could have some big surprises in store in the future, which will be discussed in Chapter 7. There is also a scientific debate about what happens to both the Greenland and Antarctic Ice Sheets beyond the next hundred years. Some scientists believe what happens in the next hundred years will determine the future of these ice sheets. One prediction suggests that though the Greenland Ice Sheet will not collapse in the next hundred years, global warming will start a process which will be irreversible and Greenland will be ice free within the next thousand years.

## What the sceptics say

One of the best ways to summarize the problems of modelling the global warming future is to review what the sceptics say, as they have many valid points and provide a basis on which our models should be improved.

1. Clouds can have a positive and negative feedback on global climate; how do we know they will not reduce the effects of global warming to a negligible amount?

As has been the case since the very first IPCC 1990 report, the greatest uncertainty in future predictions is the role of the clouds and their interaction with radiation. Clouds can both absorb and reflect radiation, thereby cooling the surface, and absorb and emit long-wave radiation, thus warming the surface. The competition between these effects depends on a number of factors: height, thickness, and radiative properties of clouds. The radiative properties and formation and development of clouds depend on the distribution of atmospheric water vapour, water drops, ice particles, atmospheric aerosols, and cloud thickness. The physical basis of how clouds are represented or parametrized in the AOGCMs has greatly improved through the inclusion of bulk representations of cloud microphysical properties in the cloud water budget equations. However, clouds still represent a significant source of potential error in climate simulations. It is still controversial whether clouds help warm or cool the planet and both situations are found in the various AOGCMs. However, it is interesting that even in those AOGCMs in which clouds cause a cooling effect, this effect is not strong enough to counter the other warming trends.

2. Different models give different results so how can we trust any of them?

This is a frequent response from many people not familiar with modelling, as there is a feeling that somehow science must be able to predict an exact future. However, in no other walk of life do we expect this exactness. For example, you would never expect to get a perfect prediction of which horse will win a race or which football team will emerge triumphant. The truth is that none of the climate models is exactly right. But what they provide is the best estimate that we have of the future. Now this view of the future is strengthened by the use of more than one model, because each model has been developed by different groups of scientists around the world, using different assumptions and different computers, and thus they provide their own particular future prediction. What causes scientists to have confidence in the model results is that they all roughly predict the same trend in global temperature and sea level for the next hundred years. Another strength of this approach is that scientists can also give you an estimation of how confident they are in the model results and also a range of possible predictions. The day that scientists give an exact estimate of what is going to happen and when is the day they will lose all credibility, rather like being told to invest in the USA stock market just before the 1929 crash as stock markets can never go down, or being sold a mortgage in the early 1980s in the UK and being told that there is no way the housing market will crash.

3. Climate models fail to predict abrupt weather conditions.

AOGCMs are not able to predict abrupt weather events because their spatial resolution is too coarse; for example, the whole of the British Isles is represented by ten points. This has led to the accusation by the sceptics that the random or chaotic factors which influence our day-to-day weather must also influence our climate. It has been known since the late 1960s that weather patterns are chaotic, as the Earth's climate system is sensitive to extremely small perturbations in initial conditions. For example, extremely slight changes in air pressure over the USA have an influence on the direction and duration of a hurricane. We all know that this sensitivity limits predictability of detailed weather forecasts to about two weeks; sometimes it feels like two days. However, predictability of climate is not limited in the same way as the prediction of the weather because the longer-term systematic influences on the atmosphere are not reliant on the initial conditions. So the longer-term trends in regional and global climate are not controlled by small-scale influences. However, what the global warming sceptics are correct about is that at present we cannot model 'non-linear events', or so-called abrupt climate changes that may occur in the future. These potential surprises are discussed in Chapter 7.

4. Climate models fail to reconstruct or predict natural variability.

The global climate system contains cyclic variations which occur on a decade or sub-decade timescale. The most famous is El Niño, which is a change in both ocean and atmospheric circulation in the Pacific region occurring every three to seven years and has a major influence on the rest of the global climate. Sceptics argue that climate models have been unable to simulate satisfactorily these events in the past. However, climate models have become increasingly good at reconstructing these past variations in El Niño–Southern Oscillation (ENSO), North Atlantic Oscillation (NAO), and related Arctic Oscillation (AO) as there has been an increasing realization that these have a profound impact upon regional climate (see Chapter 6, El Niño–Southern Oscillation section for further details). Most models are able to depict these natural variations, picking out particularly the 1976 climate shift which occurred in the Pacific Ocean. All the AOGCMs have predicted outcomes for ENSO and NAO for the next hundred years. However, a lot of improvement is required before there will be confidence in the model predictions. It is, though, testament to the realism of the AOGCMs that they can indeed reconstruct and predict future trends in these short-term oscillations.

5. The thermohaline circulation is not properly characterized in the climate models.

The deep-ocean, or thermohaline, circulation (THC) of the world's oceans is one of the basic building blocks of the coupled Atmosphere–Ocean GCMs, hence the simulations of the thermohaline circulation for the present day and the past are very good. However, uncertainties concerning the modelling of the future of the THC come from the complexities controlling deep-water formation, including the interplay in the large-scale atmospheric forcing between the warming and evaporation in the low latitudes and cooling and increased precipitation at high latitudes. In addition, ENSO can play a part by altering the freshwater balance of the tropical Atlantic. Add to this the uncertainties in the representation both of the small-scale flows over sills and through narrow straits and of ocean convection, which further limit the ability of the models to simulate situations involving substantial change in the THC. Hence most future predictions from AOGCMs have a similar THC to the present. As we will see in Chapter 7, this assumption could be completely wrong.

6. AOGCMs fail to reconstruct past climate, particularly the last ice age.

Past climates are an important test for global climate models. The biggest climate shift, for which we have many climate reconstructions, is that of the last ice age, which ended about 10,000 years ago. A comparison between palaeoclimate data for the most extreme stage of the ice age, which occurred 18,000 years ago, suggests that the global climate models are rather conservative. In fact, the best model reconstructions show only three-quarters of the climatic changes reconstructed from proxy data. Instead of invalidating our climate models, it first shows that with the extreme condition of an ice age – sea level 120 m lower, 3 km high ice sheets on America and Europe, atmospheric carbon dioxide a third lower, and atmospheric methane halved – the models can get it about 75% right. The second important observation is that the models are conservative, and they systematically underestimated the climatic changes. This means we can assume that the future climate predictions are also conservative and thus climate change is very likely to be at the top end of the estimates.

7. Galactic cosmic rays (GCRs) are ignored in the current climate models, which invalidates the models.

Galactic cosmic rays are high-energy particles that cause ionization in the atmosphere and may, therefore, affect cloud formation. GCRs vary inversely with solar variability because of the effect of solar wind. This is an excellent example of how climate science progresses by discovering new knowledge and, if it is important enough, adding it into the climate models. Very little is known about this newly discovered external forcing, GCRs, so research is continuing into this phenomenon to see if it has a large enough effect to be included in the climate models. Unfortunately it affects one of the least well-understood processes in our climate system – that of cloud formation. But the discovery that GCRs may influence climate does not invalidate the climate models, because it is all part of the progressive nature of science. We do not know everything about the climate system and we never will. Our understanding will continually improve as science progresses. Hence, model predictions of the future are continually improving. It should, however, be remembered that these models are based on the present understanding of the climate system and will always change in the future.

# Chapter 6:

# What are the possible future impacts of global warming?

As discussed in previous chapters, there is strong evidence to suggest that humanity's greenhouse gas emissions have already started to influence our climate. The most sophisticated and powerful computer models suggest global warming will cause major climatic changes by the end of the 21st century. These changes will potentially have wide-ranging effects on the natural environment as well as on human societies and our economies. Estimates have been made concerning the potential direct impacts on various socio-economic sectors, but in reality the full consequences are complicated to predict because impacts on one sector have an indirect effect on others. To assess these potential impacts, it is necessary to estimate the extent and magnitude of climate change, especially at national and local levels. For example, the latest IPCC 2001 reports look at the impacts on a continental level. There are also a number of excellent national reports, such as the National Assessment Synthesis Team 2001, which assesses climate change in the United States, dealing with the impacts on a region-by-region basis. Although much progress has been made in understanding the climate system and climate change, it must be remembered that projections of climate change and its impacts still contain huge uncertainties, particularly at the regional and local levels. The single biggest problem with global warming is our inability to predict the future. Although it is clear that humanity can live, survive, and even flourish in extreme climates from the Arctic to the Sahara, what causes problems is when the predictable extremes of the local climate are exceeded. Many of the future climate change problems are associated with water, either too much or too little compared with the usually expected amount. Unfortunately, changes in precipitation are even harder to predict than temperature. However, the most important influence on the relative impact of global warming-induced climate change is how regional economies develop and adapt in the future. So all the impacts discussed below can be mitigated to a significant degree by changes in the global economy.

The IPCC 2001 report estimates that global mean surface temperature could rise by between 1.4 and 5.8° C by 2100, which would mean that, in addition, global mean sea level would rise between 20 and 88 cm by 2100. Future climate change will have impacts on all factors affecting human society, including coastal regions, storms and floods, health and water resources, agriculture, and biodiversity. Below are reviewed each of these key areas of concern and the possible impact of climate change as assessed by the IPCC. What cannot be assessed are the impacts if climate change occurs abruptly. This is discussed in Chapter 7.

## Coastline

As we have seen, the IPCC reports that under a business-as-usual scenario (i.e. continued increase of burning fossil fuels) sea level could rise between 20 and 88 cm in the next 100 years, primarily through the thermal expansion of the oceans. This is a major concern to all coastal areas as it will decrease the effectiveness of coastal defences against storms and floods and increase the instability of cliffs and beaches. In Britain, the USA, and the rest of the developed world the response to this danger has been to add another few feet to the height of sea walls around property on the coast, the abandoning of some poorer-quality agricultural land to the sea (as it is no longer worth the expense of protecting it), and to add additional legal protection to coastal wetlands, being nature's best defence against the sea. However, globally, there are some nations based on small islands and river deltas, which face a much more dire situation.

For small island nations, such as the Maldives in the Indian Ocean and the Marshall Islands in the Pacific, a 1 m rise in sea level would flood up to 75% of the dry land, making the islands uninhabitable. Interestingly, it is also these countries, which rely on tourism, which have some of the highest fossil-fuel emissions per head of population than any other country in the world. However, there is a different twist to the story if we consider nations where a significant portion of the population lives by river deltas; these include, for example, Bangladesh, Egypt, Nigeria, and Thailand. A World Bank report in 1994 concluded that human activities on the deltas, such as freshwater extraction, were causing these areas to sink much faster than any predicted rise in sea level, increasing their vulnerability to storms and floods.

In the case of Bangladesh, over three-quarters of the country is within the deltaic region formed by the confluence of the Ganges, Brahmaputra, and Meghna rivers. Over half the country lies less than 5 m above sea level; thus flooding is a common occurrence. During the summer monsoon a quarter of the country is flooded. Yet these floods, like those of the Nile, bring with them life as well as destruction. The water irrigates and the silt fertilizes the land. The fertile Bengal Delta supports one of the world's most dense populations, over 110 million people in 140 thousand square kilometres. But the monsoon floods have been getting worse throughout the 1990s. Every year the Bengal Delta should receive over 1 billion tonnes of sediment and a thousand cubic kilometres of freshwater. This sediment load balances the erosion of the delta both by natural processes and human activity. However, the Ganges River has been diverted in India into the Hooghly Channel for irrigation. The reduced sediment input is causing the delta to subside. Exacerbating this is the rapid extraction of fresh water

26. Flooding of Bangladesh in 1998. These scenes could be more common with sea-level rise and heavier monsoons

from the delta for agriculture and drinking water. In the 1980s, 100,000 tube wells and 20,000 deep wells were sunk, increasing the freshwater extraction sixfold. Both these projects are essential to improving the quality of life for people in this region but have produced a subsidence rate of up to 2.5 centimetres per year, one of the highest rates in the world. Using estimates of subsidence rate and global warming sea-level rise, the World Bank has estimated that by the end of the 21st century the relative sea level in Bangladesh could rise by as much as 1.8 metres. In a worst-case scenario they estimated that this would result in a loss of up to 16% of land, supporting 13% of the population, and producing 12% of the current gross domestic product (GDP). Unfortunately, this scenario does not take any account of the devastation of the mangrove forest and the associated fisheries. Moreover, increased landward intrusions of salt water would further damage water quality and agriculture. This is a worst-case scenario and the greater part of the relative sea-level rise is not caused by global warming.

Another example of a threatened coastline is the Nile Delta, which is one of the oldest intensely cultivated areas on Earth. It is very heavily populated, with population densities up to 1,600 inhabitants per square kilometre. Deserts surround the low-lying, fertile floodplains. Only 2.5% of Egypt's land area, the Nile Delta and the Nile valley, are suitable for intensive agriculture. Most of a 50 km wide land strip along the coast is less than 2 m above sea level and is only protected from flooding by a 1–10 km wide coastal sand belt, shaped by discharge of the Rosetta and Damietta branches of the Nile. Erosion of the protective sand belt is a serious problem and has accelerated since the construction of the Aswan dam in the south of Egypt. A rising sea level would destroy weak parts of the sand belt, which are essential for the protection of lagoons and the low-lying reclaimed lands. These impacts could be very serious. About one-third of Egypt's fish catches are made in the lagoons, and sea-level rise would change the water quality and affect most freshwater fish; valuable agricultural land would be inundated; vital, low-lying installations in Alexandria and Port Said would be threatened; recreational tourism beach facilities would be endangered; and essential groundwater would be salinated. All these effects are preventable, as dykes and protective measures would stop the worst flooding up to a 50 cm sea-level rise. However, there may still be serious groundwater salination and the impact of increasing wave action would be serious.

The most important influence on the impact of sea-level rise on coastal regions is the rate of change. At the moment the predicted rise of about 50 cm in the next hundred years can be dealt with if there is the economic foresight to plan for the protection and adaptation of coastal regions. This then comes back to the development of regional economies and the availability of resources to implement appropriate changes. If sea level rises by over 1 m in the next hundred years, which is thought to be unlikely according to IPCC, then humanity would have major problems adapting to it.

## Storms and floods

Storms and floods are major natural hazards, which between 1951 and 1999 were responsible for 76% of the global insured losses, 58% of the economic losses, and 52% of fatalities from natural catastrophes. It is, therefore, essential we know what is likely to happen in the future. We know from historic records that during periods of rapid climate change, weather patterns can become erratic and the number of storms can increase. One example of this is the Little Ice Age, which lasted from the end of the 16th to the beginning of the 18th century, and is mainly remembered for the ice fairs that were held on the frozen River Thames. However, what is not remembered is that going into and coming out of the Little Ice Age there were some apocalyptic tempests in Europe. For example, at the end of Little Ice Age, as climate was finally warming in 1703, there was the worst recorded storm in British history, which killed over 8,000 people. There is some evidence that the temperate regions, particularly in the northern hemisphere, have become more stormy over the last fifty years. The model simulations for the future of mid-latitude storms differ widely for the next hundred years. The computer models do, however, suggest that the proportion of rainfall occurring as heavy rainfall has and will continue to increase, as will the year-to-year variability. This will increase the frequency of flooding events.

Two-fifths of the world's population lives under the monsoon belt which brings life-giving rains. Monsoons are driven by the temperature contrast between continents and oceans. For example, moisture-laden surface air blows from the Indian Ocean to the Asian continent and from the Atlantic Ocean into West Africa during northern hemisphere summers, when the land masses become much warmer than the adjacent ocean. In winter the continents become colder than the adjacent oceans and high pressure develops at the surface, causing surface winds to blow towards the ocean. Climate models indicate an increase in the strength of the summer monsoons as a result of global warming over the next hundred years. There are three reasons to support why this should occur. (1) Global warming will cause continents to warm more than the ocean in summer and this is the primary driving force of the monsoon system. (2) Decreased snow cover on Tibet, expected in a warmer world, will increase this temperature difference between land and sea, increasing the strength of the Asian summer. (3) Warmer climate means the air can hold more water vapour, so the monsoon winds will be able to carry more moisture. For the Asian summer monsoon this could mean an increase of 10–20% in average rainfall, with an interannual variability of 25–100% and a dramatic increase in the number of days with heavy rain. The most worrying model finding is the predicted increase in rain variability between years, which could double, making it very difficult to predict how much rainfall will occur each year – essential knowledge for farmers. An exception to this increase is given by the Met Office Hadley Centre GCM which predicts reduced rainfall over Amazonia, but increased rainfall in the other monsoon systems. This case study is discussed in more detail in the next chapter.

The good news is that currently there is no evidence from the last hundred years to show any increase in the number of hurricanes or cyclones. Most model predictions about future frequency and intensity of hurricanes are ambivalent, some suggesting increases while others suggest decreases. Most suggest that decadal and multi-decade variations will be larger than any trend caused by global warming.

Even if the numbers and the intensity of hurricanes and extra-tropical cyclones do not increase in the next century, global warming may influence our ability to predict these events, because our predictive capability is based on both the fundamental physics of the climate system and repetitive patterns of past weather events. For example, storms are given a return time based on their frequency in the past. This provides a means of managing coastal defences, river flood control, and water reserves. If these return times become unpredictable, then new methods will have to be adopted to deal with storm and flood events. This view is supported by many of the climate models, which show that in a warmer world the year-to-year variability of storm occurrence and other extreme climate events becomes larger. A possible example of this was in the winter of 2000 when Britain experienced two floods in one month, both of which were classified as one-in-30-year events. Again, the low cost option in most developed countries for dealing with this increased variability is better weather prediction, tighter building regulations, stricter controls on the use of coastal regions and flood plains, and greater protection for coastal wetlands.

In terms of loss of human life, the frequency and intensity of storms are not the only controlling factors. The single major control on the number of deaths and cost of damage of a storm is the level of development of the region or country that is affected. This is shown by comparing two of the worst hurricanes that hit in the 1990s. In

August 1992 Hurricane Andrew hit the United States and caused record damage, estimated at $20 billion, but killed only 53 people. In 1998 Hurricane Mitch hit Central America and killed at least 20,000 people, made 2 million people homeless, and set back the economic growth of the region by decades. Therefore, even if global warming does increase the number of storms globally, economic development of the poorer countries could very quickly reduce the death rate but of course correspondingly increase the cost of the associated damage.

## El Niño–Southern Oscillation

One of the most important and mysterious elements in global climate is the periodic switching of the direction and intensity of ocean currents and winds in the Pacific. Originally known as El Niño ('Christ child' in Spanish), as it usually appears at Christmas, and now more normally known as ENSO (El Niño–Southern Oscillation), this phenomenon typically occurs every three to seven years. It may last from several months to more than a year. The 1997–8 El Niño conditions were the strongest on record and caused droughts in southern USA, East Africa, northern India, north-east Brazil, and Australia. In Indonesia, forest fires burned out of control in the very dry conditions. In California, parts of South America, Sri Lanka, and east-central Africa there were torrential rains and terrible floods.

ENSO is an oscillation between three climates, the 'normal' conditions, La Niña, and 'El Niño' (see Figure 27). El Niño conditions have been linked to changes in the monsoon, storm patterns, and occurrence of droughts all over the world. The state of the ENSO has also been linked to the position and occurrence of hurricanes in the Atlantic. For example, it is thought that the poor prediction of where Hurricane Mitch made landfall was because the ENSO conditions were not considered and the strong trade winds helped drag the storm south across Central America instead of west as predicted.

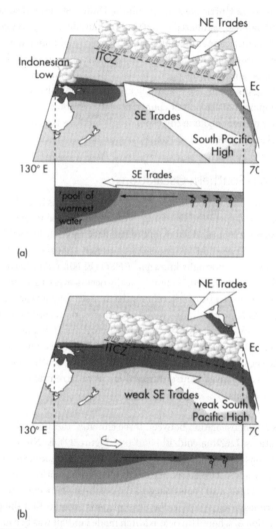

27. El Niño – Southern Oscillation (ENSO) a) normal conditions and b) El Niño conditions

Predicting El Niño events is very difficult but getting steadily better. For example, there is now a large network of both ocean and satellite monitoring systems over the Pacific Ocean, primarily aimed at recording sea-surface temperature, which is the major indicator of the state of the ENSO. By using this climatic data in both computer circulation models and statistical models, predictions are made of the likelihood of an El Niño or La Niña event. We are really still in the infancy stage of developing our understanding and predictive capabilities of the ENSO phenomenon.

There is also considerable debate over whether ENSO has been affected by global warming. The El Niño conditions generally occur every three to seven years; however, they have returned for three years out of four: 1991–2, 1993–4, and 1994–5. El Niño then returned again to wreak havoc on global weather in 1997–8. Reconstruction of past climate using coral reefs in the western Pacific shows sea-surface temperature variations back 150 years, well beyond our historic records. The sea-surface temperature shows the shifts in ocean current, which accompany shifts in the ENSO and reveal that there have been two major changes in the frequency and intensity of El Niño events. First, was a shift at the beginning of the 20th century from a 10–15-year cycle to a 3–5-year cycle. The second shift was a sharp threshold in 1976 when a marked shift to more intense and even more frequent El Niño events occurred. These are sobering results considering the huge weather disruption and disasters caused by recent El Niño events. Modelling results also suggest that the current 'heightened' state of El Niño can permanently shift weather patterns. For example, it seems that the drought region in the USA could be shifting eastward. However, as we have seen, to predict an El Niño event six months from now is hard enough without trying to assess whether or not ENSO is going to get more extreme over the next 100 years. Most computer models of ENSO in the future are inconclusive; some have found an increase and others have found none. This is, therefore, one part of the climate system which we do not know how global warming will affect. Not only does ENSO have a direct impact on global climate but it also affects the numbers, intensity, and pathways of hurricanes and cyclones, and the strength and timing of the Asian monsoon. Hence, when discussing the potential impacts of global warming one of the largest unknowns is the variation of ENSO and its knock-on effects on the rest of the global climate system.

Another possibility that we must consider is that in the early Holocene no evidence has been found for ENSO. In fact, it is thought that ENSO began sometime between 4,000 and 5,000 years ago. So Bjørn Lomborg radically suggests in his book *The Skeptical Environmentalist* that a 2–3°C warming could be a good thing for the future as it may switch off ENSO. None of the computer models used to look at future climate has found this effect, and it must be remembered that the position of the Earth's orbit compared to the sun was very different in the early Holocene, but it is something else to consider.

## Health

It has been suggested that global warming will have an adverse effect on human health. Initial suggestions have been that increased global temperatures will increase the death rate. A recent study shows that the population in Europe has successfully adapted their lifestyle to take into consideration the high summer temperatures. This is a classic case of individual risk assessment and adaptation, because most heat-related mortality occurs when the temperature goes above a usual temperature. For example, in London heat-related mortality starts at 22.3°C while in Athens it starts at 25.7°C. So it seems that providing the correct information and continued increased accessibility to air conditioning will mean that the world will be able to adapt to warmer conditions. In fact, it has also been suggested that the death rate may even drop, since more people die from cold weather than warm weather, thus warmer winters would reduce this cause of death.

By far the most important threat to human health, however, is access to fresh drinking water. At present, rising human populations, particularly growing concentrations in urban areas, are putting great stress on water resources. The impacts of climate change – including changes in temperature, precipitation, and sea levels – are expected to have varying consequences for the availability of fresh water around the world. For example, changes in river run-off will affect the yields of rivers and reservoirs and thus the recharging of groundwater supplies. An increase in the rate of evaporation will also affect water supplies and contribute to the salinization of irrigated agricultural lands. Rising sea levels may result in saline intrusion in coastal aquifers. Currently, approximately 1.7 billion people, a third of the world's population, live in countries that are water-stressed. IPCC reports suggest that with the projected global population increase, and the expected climate change, assuming present consumption patterns, 5 billion people will experience water stress by 2025. Climate change is likely to have the greatest impact in countries with a high ratio of relative use to available supply. Regions with abundant water supplies will get more than they want with increased flooding. As suggested above, computer models predict much heavier rains and thus major flood problems for Europe, whilst, paradoxically, countries that currently have little water (e.g. those relying on desalinization) may be relatively unaffected. It will be countries in between, which have no history or infrastructure for dealing with water shortages, which will be the most affected. For in central Asia, North Africa, and southern Africa there will be even less rainfall and water quality will become increasingly degraded through higher temperatures and pollutant run-off. Add to this the predicted increased year-to-year variability in rainfall, and droughts will become more common. Hence, it is those countries that have been identified as most at risk which need to start planning now to conserve their water supplies and/or deal with the increased risks of flooding, because it is the lack of infrastructure to deal with drought and floods rather than the lack or abundance of water which causes the threat to human health. Therefore, economic development of areas most at risk is essential in the next century to provide resources to mitigate the effects of global warming.

Another possible future threat to human health is the increased transmission of many infectious diseases, as these are directly affected by climatic factors. Infective agents and their vector organisms (e.g. mosquitoes) are sensitive to factors such as temperature, surface water, humidity, wind, soil moisture, and changes in forest distribution. For example, there is a strong correlation between increased sea-surface temperature and sea level and the annual severity of the cholera epidemics in Bangladesh. With predicted future climate change and the rise in Bangladesh's relative sea level, cholera epidemics could increase. Climate change will particularly influence vector-borne diseases (VBD), i.e. diseases which are carried by another organism, such as malaria carried by mosquitoes. It is, therefore, projected that climate change and altered weather patterns would affect the range (both altitude and latitude), intensity, and seasonality of many vector-borne and other infectious diseases. In general, increased warmth and moisture caused by global warming will enhance transmission of diseases. While the potential transmission of many of these diseases increases in response to climate change, we should remember that our capacity to control the diseases will also change. New or improved vaccination can be expected; some vector species can be constrained by use of pesticides. Nevertheless, there are uncertainties and risks here, too: for example, long-term pesticides use breed-resistant strains and kill many predators of pests.

The most important vector-borne disease is malaria, with currently 500 million infected people worldwide, which is about twice the population of the USA. *Plasmodium vivax*, which is carried by the Anopheles mosquito, is an organism which causes malaria. The main climate factors that have a bearing on the malarial transmission potential of the mosquito population are temperature and precipitation. Assessments of the potential impact of global climate change on the incidence of malaria suggest a widespread increase of risk because of the expansion of the areas suitable for malaria transmission. Mathematical models mapping out the suitable temperature zones for mosquitoes suggest that by the 2080s the potential exposure of people could increase by 2–4% (260–320 million people). The predicted increase is most pronounced at the borders of endemic malarial areas and at higher altitudes within malarial areas. The changes in malaria risk must be interpreted on the basis of local environmental conditions, the effects of socio-economic development, and malaria control programmes or capabilities. The incidence of infection is most sensitive to climate changes in areas of South-East Asia, South America, and parts of Africa. Global warming will also provide excellent conditions for Anopheles mosquitoes to breed in southern England, Europe, and the northern USA.

It should, however, be noted that the occurrence of most tropical diseases is related to development. An example was major epidemic disease in much of Europe during the Little Ice Age. As recently as the 1940s malaria was endemic in Finland, Poland, Russia, and 36 states in the USA including Washington, Oregon, Idaho, Montana, North Dakota, New York, Pennsylvania, and New Jersey. So though global warming has the potential to increase the range of many of these tropical diseases, the experience of Europe and the USA suggests that combating malaria is strongly linked to development and resources: development to ensure efficient monitoring of the disease and resources to secure a strong effort to eradicate the mosquitoes and their breeding grounds.

## Biodiversity

The IPCC report lists the following species as those most at threat from climate change as a result of global warming: the mountain gorilla in Africa, amphibians that only live in the cloud forests of the neotropics, the spectacled bear of the Andes, forest birds of Tanzania, the Resplendent Quetzal in Central America, the Bengal tiger, and other species only found in the Sundarban wetlands, rainfall-sensitive plants found only in the Cape Floral Kingdom of South Africa, polar bears, and penguins. Natural habitats that are threatened include coral reefs, mangroves, other coastal wetlands, mountain ecosystems found in the upper 200–300 m of mountainous areas, prairie wetlands, permafrost ecosystems, and ice edge ecosystems which provide a habitat for polar bears and penguins. The primary reason for the threat to these species or ecosystems is that they are unable to migrate in response to climate change because of their particular geographical location or the encroachment of human activity, particularly farming and urbanization. An example of the former is the cloud forests of the neotropics: as climate changes, this particular climatic zone will migrate up the mountainside until the point where there is no more mountain.

One example of an ecosystem under threat is the coral reefs. Coral reefs are a valuable economic resource for fisheries, recreation, tourism, and coastal protection. In addition, reefs are one of the largest global stores of marine biodiversity, with untapped genetic resources. Some estimate that the global cost of losing the coral reefs runs into hundreds of billions of dollars each year. The last few years have seen unprecedented declines in the health of coral reefs. In 1998 El Niño was associated with record sea-surface temperatures and associated coral bleaching, which is when the coral expels the algae that live within them and that are necessary to their survival. In some regions, as much as 70% of the coral may have died in a single season. There has also been an upsurge in the variety, incidence, and virulence of coral disease in recent years, with major die-offs in Florida and much of the Caribbean region. In addition, increasing atmospheric carbon dioxide concentrations could decrease the calcification rates of the reef-building corals, resulting in weaker skeletons, reduced growth rates, and increased vulnerability to erosion. Model results suggest these effects would be most severe at the current margins of coral reef distribution.

On a more theoretical note, a recent study by Thomas *et al.* (*Nature*,

427, 145–8, 2004) investigated the possible increase in the likely extinction rate over the next 50 years in key regions such as Mexico, Amazonia, and Australia. The theoretical models suggest that by 2050 the climatic changes predicted by the IPCC would commit 18% (warming of 0.8–1.7°C), 24% (1.8–2.0°C), and 35% (above 2.0°C) of the species studied to extinction in these regions. That means a quarter of all species in these regions may become extinct by the middle of this century. There are many assumptions in their models, which may or may not be true; for example, they assume we know the full climatic range in which each species can persist and the precise relationship between shrinking habitat and extinction rates. So these results can only be seen as the likely direction of extinction rates, not necessarily the exact magnitude. However, these predictions do represent a huge future threat to regional and global biodiversity and illustrate the sensitivity of the biological system to the amount and rate of warming that will occur in the future.

## Agriculture

One of the major worries concerning future climate change is the effect it will have on agriculture, both globally and regionally. The main question is whether the world can feed itself under the predicted future global warming conditions. Predictions of cereal production for 2060 suggest that there are still huge uncertainties about whether climate change will cause global agricultural production to increase or decrease. If the predicted temperature increases are considered, then we expect there to be a drop in food production in both the developed and less-developed countries. But if other effects are taken into consideration, then this effect of temperature is greatly reduced, or in the case of the developed world becomes an increase. One of the most important additional factors is that increased atmospheric carbon dioxide acts as a fertilizer; thus scientific studies have shown that plants in an atmosphere which contains more carbon dioxide grow faster and better, because the $CO_2$ is essential for photosynthesis and the prime source of carbon for plants. So plants like more atmospheric $CO_2$ and thus farm yields may increase in the future in many regions. In addition, if it is assumed that farmers can take action to adapt to changing climate this also boosts or at least maintains agricultural production in many regions. For example, farmers could vary the planting time and/or switch to a different variety of the same plant to respond to changing conditions. Therefore, models suggest that with reasonable assumptions on a worldwide scale, the change is expected to be small or moderate. But this does not mean the amount of cereal produced worldwide will be the same or lower in 2060 compared with today. Since 1960 world grain production has doubled and is predicted to continue to rise at a similar rate. So even a pessimistic 1999 study using the Met Office Hadley Centre climate model estimated that cereal production in 2080 would only increase by 90% compared with today, not by 94% which would have occurred in the absence of global warming.

This, however, masks the huge changes that will occur in different regions, with both winners and losers, the poorest countries, of course, which are least able to adapt, being the losers. Also the results of all these studies are heavily dependent on the assumed trade models and market forces used, as, unfortunately, agricultural production in the world has very little to do with feeding the world's population and much more to do with trade and economics. Hence, this is why the EU has stockpiles of food, while many underdeveloped countries export cash crops (e.g. sugar, cocoa, coffee, tea, rubber, etc.) but cannot adequately feed their own populations. A classic example is the West African state of Benin, where cotton farmers can obtain cotton yields of four to eight times per hectare greater than their US competitors in Texas. The USA subsidizes their farmers, however, which means that US cotton is cheaper than that coming from Benin. Currently, US cotton farmers receive $3.9 billion in subsidies, almost twice the total GDP of Benin. So even if global warming makes Texan cotton yields even lower, it still does not change the biased market forces.

So in the computer models, markets can reinforce the difference between agricultural impacts in developed and developing countries and, depending on the trade model used, agricultural exporters may gain in money even though the supplies fall, because when a product becomes scarce the price rises. The other completely unknown factor is the extent to which a country's agriculture can be adaptable. For example, the models assume that production levels in developing countries will fall more compared with those in the developed countries because their estimated capability to adapt is less than that of developed countries. But this is just another assumption that has no analogue in the past, and as these effects on agriculture will occur over the next century, many developing countries may catch up with the developed world in terms of adaptability.

One example of the real regional problems that global warming could cause is the case of coffee-growing in Uganda. Here, the total area suitable for growing Robusta coffee would be dramatically reduced, to less than 10%, by a temperature increase of 2°C. Only higher areas would remain; the rest would become too hot to grow coffee. This demonstrates the vulnerability to the effects of global warming of many developing countries, whose economies often rely heavily on one or two agricultural products. Hence, one major adaptation to global warming should be the broadening of the economic and agricultural base of the most threatened countries. This, of course, is much harder to do in practice than on paper and it is clear that the EU and US agricultural subsidies and the current one-sided World Trade Agreements have a greater effect on global agricultural production and the ability of countries to feed themselves than global warming will ever have.

# Chapter 7
# Surprises

All the impacts discussed above assume that there is a linear relationship between greenhouse gas forcing and climate change, as produced by the AOGCMs. There is, however, increasing concern among scientists that climate change may occur abruptly. This is because there is recent scientific evidence that many past climatic changes have occurred with startling speed. For example, ice-core records suggest that half the warming in Greenland since the last ice age was achieved in only a decade. Some of these regional changes involved temperature changes of over 10°C. This relates back to Chapter 1 and the discussion of how climate changes, whether it varies smoothly or contains thresholds and bifurcations. Such is the concern that future climate change may be abrupt that in 2003 the prestigious Royal Society in London convened a conference and an associated report on this very topic, while the National Research Council in the USA commissioned a report on Abrupt Climate Change, published in 2002. Though this is a new paradigm, the ability of the global climate system to change abruptly has been well established by research over the last decade. What both reports stress is the need for the wider community of natural and social scientists, as well as policy makers, to recognize this new paradigm and act accordingly. The National Research Council (NRC) Report makes five recommendations:

1. Improve the fundamental knowledge base related to abrupt climate change.

Below I review three possible abrupt climate surprises: deep-ocean circulation, gas hydrates, and Amazonia. But what connects them all is that we really do not know how the global climate will react to global warming in the future. It is thus essential for more work to be done on how abruptly these changes occur. Moreover, the NRC report suggests there is need for more understanding of how the global and regional economies would deal with abrupt climate change.

2. Improve modelling focused on abrupt climate change.

At the moment most models try to achieve a steady-state or equilibrium between the forcing and the variations. What is required is a new type of high-resolution model to look at how easily abrupt climate change can occur. The NRC report stressed that new possible mechanisms of abrupt climate change should be investigated and a hierarchy of models will be required, since many of these abrupt changes are initiated at the fine spatial scale, which AOGCMs are currently unable to simulate.

3. Improve palaeoclimatic data related to abrupt climate change.

Past climate changes have provided us with many of the clues about how future climate could change. For example, oceanographers had not considered the idea that the deep-ocean circulation could change until it was shown that it was radically different during the last ice age. The NRC report suggests that improvement is required in both geographical and temporal resolution of abrupt events in the past. Also there is a need to focus on water, both too much (floods) and too little (droughts), as these are by far the most important influences on humanity.

4. Improve statistical approaches.

This has been mentioned before in this book, but current practice in climate statistics is to assume a simple unchanging distribution of outcomes. For example, a one-in-30-year storm will statistically always occur once in 30 years. This assumption leads to serious underestimation of the likelihood of extreme events; hence the conceptual basis and application of climate statistics should be re-examined, particularly as all future predictions are that the year-to-year variability in extreme weather will increase in the future.

5. Investigate 'no-regrets' strategies to reduce vulnerability.

The NRC report stresses that research should be undertaken to identify 'no-regrets' measures to reduce vulnerabilities and increase adaptive capacity at little or no cost. No-regrets measures may include low-cost steps to slow climate change, improve climate forecasting, slow biodiversity loss, improve water, land, and air quality. Technological changes, such as clean technology, may increase the adaptability and resiliency of both economic and ecological systems faced with abrupt climate change. The report stresses the need for research into how poor countries can be assisted to develop a more adaptable scientific and economic infrastructure to reduce the effects of abrupt climate change.

Below, I discuss just three possible 'surprises' that could occur in the next hundred years because of global warming. What is common to all these hypotheses is that we really have no idea if and when they will happen and, if they do, what will be the effects.

## Deep-ocean circulation

The circulation of the ocean is one of the major controls on our global climate. In fact, the deep ocean is the only candidate for driving and sustaining internal long-term climate change (of hundreds to thousands of years) because of its volume, heat capacity, and inertia. In the North Atlantic, the north-east trending Gulf Stream carries warm and salty surface water from the Gulf of

Mexico up to the Nordic seas (Figure 28). The increased saltiness or salinity in the Gulf Stream is due to the huge amount of evaporation that occurs in the Caribbean, which removes moisture from the surface waters and concentrates the salts in the seawater. As the Gulf Stream flows northward it cools down. The combination of a high salt content and low temperature makes the surface water heavier or denser. Hence, when it reaches the relatively fresh oceans north of Iceland, the surface water has cooled sufficiently to become dense enough to sink into the deep ocean. The 'pull' exerted by the sinking of this dense water mass helps maintain the strength of the warm Gulf Stream, ensuring a current of warm tropical water flowing into the north-east Atlantic, sending mild air masses across to the European continent. It has been calculated that the Gulf Stream delivers 27,000 times the energy of all of Britain's power stations put together. If you are in any doubt about how good the Gulf Stream is for the European climate, compare the winters at the same latitude on either side of the Atlantic Ocean, for example, London with Labrador or Lisbon with New York. Or a better comparison is between Western Europe and the West coast of North America, which have a similar geographical relationship between the ocean and continent. So think of Alaska and Scotland which are at about the same latitude.

The newly formed deep water sinks to a depth of between 2,000 and 3,500 m in the ocean and flows southward down the Atlantic Ocean, as the North Atlantic Deep Water (NADW). In the South Atlantic Ocean it meets a second type of deep water, which is formed in the Southern Ocean and is called the Antarctic Bottom Water (AABW). This is formed in a different way to NADW. Antarctica is surrounded by sea ice and deep water forms in coast polnyas or large holes in the sea ice. Out-blowing Antarctic winds push sea ice away from the continental edge to produce these holes. The winds are so cold that they super-cool the exposed surface waters. This leads to more sea-ice formation and salt rejection, producing the coldest and saltiest water in the world. AABW flows around the

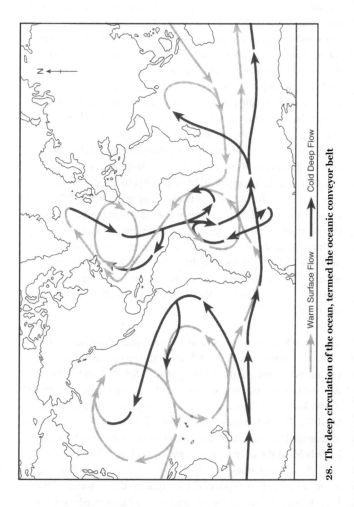

28. **The deep circulation of the ocean, termed the oceanic conveyor belt**

Warm Surface Flow →     Cold Deep Flow →

Antarctic and penetrates the North Atlantic, flowing under the warmer and thus somewhat lighter NADW (Figure 29a). The AABW also flows into both the Indian and Pacific Oceans.

This balance between the NADW and AABW is extremely important in maintaining our present climate, as not only does it keep the Gulf Stream flowing past Europe but it maintains the right amount of heat exchange between the northern and southern hemispheres. Scientists have shown that the circulation of deep water can be weakened or 'switched off' if there is enough input of fresh water to make the surface water too light to sink. This evidence has come from both computer models and the study of past climates. Scientists have coined the phrase 'dedensification' to mean the removal of density by adding fresh water and/or warming up the water, both of which prevent seawater from being dense enough to sink. As we have seen, there is already concern that global warming will cause significant melting of the polar ice caps. This will lead to more fresh water being added to the polar oceans. Global warming could, therefore, cause the collapse of NADW, and a weakening of the warm Gulf Stream (Figure 29b). This would cause much colder European winters, stormier conditions, and more severe weather. However, the influence of the warm Gulf Stream is mainly in the winter so it does not affect summer temperatures. So, if the Gulf Stream fails, global warming would still cause European summers to heat up. Europe would end up with extreme seasonal weather.

A counter scenario is that if the Antarctic ice sheet starts to melt significantly before the Greenland and Arctic ice, things could be very different. If enough melt-water is put in the Southern Ocean then AABW will be severely curtailed. Because the deep-water system is a balancing act between NADW and AABW, if AABW is reduced then the NADW will increase and expand (Figure 29c). The problem is that NADW is warmer than AABW, and because if you heat up a liquid it expands, the NADW will take up more space. So any increase in NADW will mean an increase in sea level. Computer

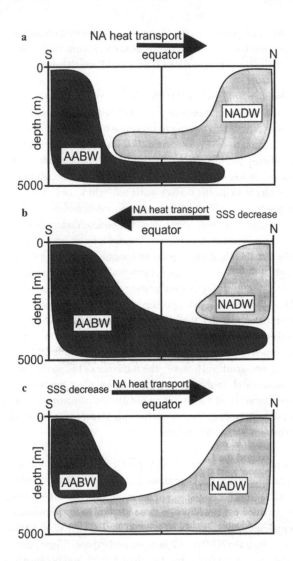

29. **Different possible circulation of the deep ocean depending sea surface salinity (SSS), i.e., freshwater input**

models by Professor Seidov (Penn State University, USA) and myself have suggested that a melt-water event in the Southern Ocean could cause a reduction in the AABW and the expansion of the NADW, and would result in an average sea-level increase of 2.5 m (Figure 30). The problem is that we have no idea how much fresh water it will take to shut off either the NADW or the AABW. Nor at the moment can we predict which will melt first, the Arctic or Antarctic. We do know that these events have happened frequently in the past and have drastically altered the global climate. If global warming continues, some time in the future enough melt-water will be generated and the options will be either severe alteration of the European climate or an additional 2.5 m of global sea-level rise.

Not only do we not know how much fresh water is required to reduce either North Atlantic or Southern Ocean deep-water formation, we are also not sure whether it could be reversed. This is because computer models suggest the freshwater–deep-ocean system could be a threshold-bifurcated system. Figure 31 demonstrates this bifurcation of the climate system and shows that there can be different relationships between climate and the forcing mechanism, depending on the direction of the threshold. The bifurcation system is very common in natural systems, for example, in cases where inertia or the shift between different states of matter need to be overcome. Figure 31 shows that in cases A and B the system is reversible, but in case C it is not. In case C the control variable must increase to more than it was in the previous equilibrium state to get over the threshold and return the system to its pre-threshold state. Let us consider this in terms of the salinity of the North Atlantic versus the production of North Atlantic Deep Water (NADW). We know that adding more fresh water to the North Atlantic hampers the production of salty cold, and hence heavy deep water. In case A, changing the salinity of the North Atlantic has no effect on the amount of NADW produced. It is a very insensitive system. In case B, reducing the salinity reduces the production of NADW; however, if the salt is replaced, then the

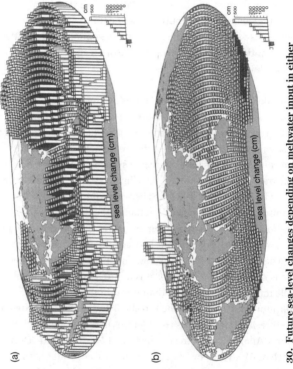

(a)

cm
500

250
200
150
100
50
0

sea level change (cm)

(b)

cm
500

250
200
150
100
50
0

sea level change (cm)

30. Future sea-level changes depending on meltwater input in either
a) Southern Ocean around Antartica or b) North Atlantic Ocean

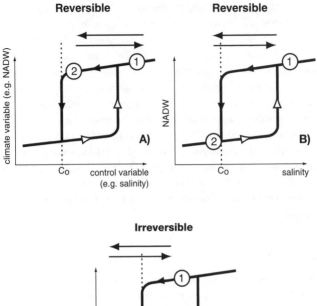

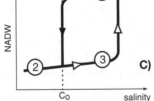

**31. Bifurcation of the climate system**

production of NADW returns to its previous, pre-threshold level. In case C, reducing the North Atlantic salinity reduces the production of NADW. However, simply returning the same amount of salt does not return the NADW production to the normal level. Because of the bifurcation, a lot more salt has to be injected to bring back the NADW production to its previous level (see Figures 5*e* and 29*c*). It may be that the extra amount of salt required is not possible within the system and so this makes the system theoretically irreversible. The major problems we face when looking at future climate change is whether a bifurcation system exists and whether the system will go beyond a point of being reversible. What is worrying is that these threshold systems can apply to any part of the climate system. Another example is the position of the monsoons: in Oman and other parts of Arabia fresh groundwater has been dated to 18,000 years ago, to the last ice age; none of it is any younger. This suggests that under glacial conditions the modern South-East Asian monsoon belt came much further north, producing significant rains in what are now extremely arid regions. As soon as the global climate moved into an interglacial the monsoons shifted. The next question is: if global warming changes the position of the monsoons again, will they return to the present position if the effects of global warming lessen?

## Gas hydrates

Currently, below the world's oceans and permafrost lurks a deadly threat – gas hydrates. These are a mixture of water and methane, which is sustained as a solid at very low temperatures and very high pressures. These gas hydrates are a solid composed of a cage of water molecules, which hold individual molecules of methane and other gases. The methane comes from decaying organic matter found deep in ocean sediments and in soils beneath permafrost. These gas hydrate reservoirs are extremely unstable, as a slight increase in temperature or decrease in pressure can cause them to destabilize and thus pose a major risk. The impacts of global warming include the heating up of both the oceans and the permafrost, which could cause the gas hydrates to break down, pumping out huge amounts of methane into the atmosphere. Methane is a very strong greenhouse gas, 21 times more powerful than carbon dioxide. If enough were released it would raise temperatures even more, releasing even more gas hydrates – producing a runaway greenhouse effect. There are 10,000 gigatonnes of gas hydrates stored beneath our feet compared with only 180 gigatonnes of carbon dioxide currently in the atmosphere.

The reason why scientists are so worried about this is because there is evidence that a runaway greenhouse effect occurred 55 million years ago. During this hot-house event 1,200 gigatonnes of gas hydrates were released, but it accelerated the natural greenhouse effect, producing an extra 5°C of warming. Scientists are, however, divided on whether global warming will cause a significant release of gas hydrates. The reason is that there are two controls on oceanic gas hydrates: one is temperature and the other is pressure or sea level. However, model calculations by Peter Cox at the Met Office Hadley Centre suggest that at current predicted rates of global warming, sea level will not rise faster to counter the effects of the warming ocean, hence gas hydrates will start to break down in the next hundred years, releasing methane.

There is another problem. If significant parts of the Greenland and Antarctica Ice Sheets melt, the removal of ice from the continent means that it will recover and start to move upwards. This isostatic rebound can be seen in the British Isles, which are still recovering from the last ice age, with Scotland still rising while England is lowering. This will mean that the relative sea level around the continental shelf will fall, removing the weight and thus the pressure of the sea water on the marine sediment. Pressure removal is a much more efficient way of destabilizing gas hydrates than temperature increases and so huge amounts of methane could be released from around the Arctic and Antarctic. There is another secondary effect of gas hydrate release: when the hydrates break down they can do so explosively. There is clear evidence in the past that violent gas hydrate releases have caused massive slumping of the continental shelf and associated tsunamis (giant waves). The most famous is the Norwegian Storegga slide which occurred about 8,000 years ago, was the size of Wales, and produced a 15 m high tsunami, which wiped out many prehistoric settlements in Scotland. Hence, we cannot rule out the fact that global warming could lead to an increased frequency of gas hydrate-generated submarine landslides and thus tsunamis of over 15 m in height hitting our coasts. Up to now, only the countries around the Pacific rim are prepared for this type of event as many of these tsunamis are set off by earthquakes. But gas hydrate-generated tsunamis could occur anywhere in the ocean.

## Amazonia

In 1542 Francisco de Orellana led the first European voyage down the Amazon River. During this intrepid voyage the expedition met a lot of resistance from the local Indians; in one particular tribe the women warriors were so fierce that they drove their male warriors in front of them with spears. Thus the river was named after the famous women warriors of the Greek myths, the Amazons. This makes Francisco de Orellana one of the unluckiest explorers of that age, as normally the river would have been named after him. This voyage also started our almost mystical wonder of the greatest river and the largest area of rainforest in the world, something we still feel today. The Amazon River discharges approximately 20% of all fresh water carried to the oceans. The Amazon drainage basin is the world's largest, covering an area of 7,050,000 km$^2$, about the size of Europe. The river is a product of the Amazon monsoon, which every summer brings huge rains. This also produces the spectacular expanse of rainforest, which supports one of the highest diversity and largest number of species of any area in the world. The Amazon rainforest is also important when it comes to the future of global warming, as it is a huge natural store of carbon. Up until recently it was thought that an established rainforest such as the Amazon had reached maturity and thus could not take up any more carbon dioxide. Experiments in the heart of the Amazon rainforest have shown this could be wrong and that the Amazon rainforest might be sucking up an additional 5 tonnes of atmospheric carbon dioxide per ha per year. This is because plants react favourably to increased carbon dioxide; because it is the raw material for photosynthesis, the more of it the better. So having more carbon dioxide in the atmosphere acts like a fertilizer, stimulating plant growth. Because of the size of the Amazon rainforest it seems that presently it is taking up a large percentage of our atmospheric carbon dioxide

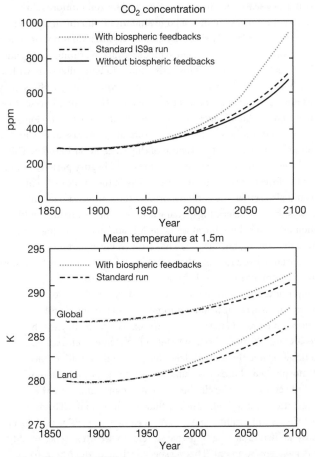

**32. Met office model of $CO_2$ concentration and mean temperature over time**

pollution, about three-quarters of the world's car pollution. But things could change in the future.

Global climate models developed at the Met Office Hadley Centre suggest that global warming by 2050 could have increased the winter dry season in Amazonia. For the Amazon rainforest to survive it requires not only a large amount of rain during the wet season but a relatively short dry season so that it does not dry out. According to the Hadley Centre model, global warming could cause the global climate to shift towards a more El Niño-like state with a much longer South American dry season. Kim Stanley Robinson in his novel *Forty Signs of Rain* uses the term Hyperniño to refer to a new climate state. Hence, the Amazon rainforest could no longer survive and would be replaced by savannah (dry grassland) which is found both to the east and south of the Amazon Basin today. This replacement would occur because the extended dry periods would lead to forest fires destroying large parts of the rainforest. This would also return the carbon stored in the rainforest back into the atmosphere, accelerating global warming. The savannah would then take over those burnt areas, as it is adapted to coping with the long dry season, but savannah has a much lower carbon storage potential per square mile than rainforest. So the Amazon rainforest at the moment might be helping to reduce the amount of pollution we put into the atmosphere, but ultimately it may cause global warming to accelerate at an unprecedented and currently unpredicted rate (Figure 32). However, we must still view this result with caution. First, the Met Office Hadley Centre model is unique, as it is the first model to have not only a fully coupled atmosphere and ocean system, but also a vegetation system which is fully coupled to the climate, so that climate influences the vegetation and the vegetation influences the climate. This is an extremely important step forward in climate models as ecologists have known for a long time that different vegetation types modify the local environment. This is especially true of the Amazon rainforest, which recycles at least 50% of the precipitation, maintaining a warm moist environment. At present there are no other GCMs to compare the results with. So until this happens we cannot place too much confidence in one model, but it does clearly indicate where we have to concentrate our scientific effort in the future. Second, the Met Office Hadley Centre model is one of many GCMs that show the world moving to a more El Niño-like state; but not all the GCMs reviewed by the IPCC show this shift. As the shift towards a more El Niño-like state is the key control on the future of the rainforest, it is something we need to have confidence in. As discussed before, confidence in science moves forward as a consequence of the weight of evidence and at the moment there is not enough convincing evidence that the world will move into a more El Niño-like state, or Robinson's Hyperniño. Third, about 80% of the release of additional carbon from the terrestrial biosphere into the atmosphere predicted in the Hadley Centre model comes from increased soil decomposition which is a poorly understood process on the global scale. So until more GCMs have coupled vegetation models we cannot have confidence in this one prediction. But, as they say, watch this space!

# Chapter 8
## Politics

The most logical approach to the global warming problem would seem to be to cut emissions significantly. Scientists have argued that significant cuts are required (up to 60%) to contain global warming to only one degree. This, however, has major implications for the world economy, and how much cutting emissions costs compared with the damage that climate change may cause is a hugely contentious issue. The UNFCCC (United Nations Framework Convention on Climate Change) was created at the Rio Earth Summit in 1992 to try to negotiate a worldwide agreement in reducing greenhouse gases and limiting the impact of global warming. Two major steps forward have been achieved in the last ten years. The first occurred at midnight on 13 Dec 1997 when the Kyoto Protocol was formed, which stated the general principles for a worldwide treaty on cutting greenhouse emissions and, more specifically, that all developed nations would aim to cut their emission by 5.2% on their 1990 levels by 2008–12. However, some countries have continued to increase their emissions significantly since 1990 and thus will have great difficulty in achieving this reduction. The second breakthrough was in Bonn on 23 July 2001, when 186 countries ratified and signed the Kyoto Protocol, making it a legal treaty. However, the USA, under the leadership of President Bush, withdrew from the climate negotiations in March 2001 and so did not sign the Kyoto Protocol at the Bonn meeting. With the USA producing about a quarter of the world's carbon dioxide pollution, this is a big blow for the treaty. Moreover, the targets set by the Kyoto Protocol were reduced during the Bonn meeting to make sure that Japan, Canada, and Australia would join. The targets for the 37 richest and most developed countries will be a cut of 1–3% compared with their 1990 levels. The treaty does not include underdeveloped countries. This is a concern, because if countries such as India and China continue to develop, they will produce huge amounts of pollution. For example, if these two countries achieve their aim to have the same car to family ratio as Europe, there will be an extra billion cars in the world.

The Kyoto Protocol entered into force on the 16th February 2005. It could only come into effect after Russia ratified the treaty, thereby meeting the requirement that at least 55 countries, representing more than 55% of the global emissions made, signed up to it. Russia's membership tipped the scales, and allowed the Kyoto Protocol to become national law. So what have the 186 nations signed up for? The 38 industrialized nations have agreed to binding targets to reduce their greenhouse gas emissions. The EU will immediately start turning the treaty into law for all member countries, forcing a cut in greenhouse emissions of 8% on the 1990 level by 2010. The United Kingdom's legal target will be 12.5%, a larger reduction to allow poorer EU countries room for development. A total of $500 million (£350 million) of new funds a year will be provided by the industrialized world to help developing countries to adapt to climate change and to provide new clean technologies. Industrial countries will also be able to plant forests, manage existing ones, and change farming practices, and thereby claim credit for removing carbon dioxide from the atmosphere. In addition, there is provision in the Kyoto Protocol concerning national and international trade in carbon emissions. Currently, countries that have emission targets will be able to trade carbon emissions within their own national economy and between each other. What has not yet been agreed is international trading with countries without emission targets, as this was initially opposed by the EU and international environmental NGOs (non-governmental organizations), but generally supported by other industrial nations and the less-developed world. There are many who want the Kyoto Protocol to go further and allow industrial nations to buy carbon credits from less-developed nations. For example, if Brazil prevents the destruction of, or reforests, an area of Amazonia, this could count as a carbon credit, which could be sold to an industrial nation to offset their required emissions reduction.

## The main contenders

Below is a Who's Who guide to the international climate talks. These different coalitions, which have formed during the climate change negotiations, provide us with some insight into the different agendas of different countries. In addition, there are strong lobbying interests from both individual states and environmental, business, and industrial groups, which are also discussed below.

### G-77 and China

The Group of 77 is the main developing country coalition and was formed in 1964 during the New International Economic Order negotiations under the UN Conference on Trade and Development (UNCTAD). China regularly allies itself with this group, which now numbers over 130 members. The country holding the annually rotating Chair of the Group 77 in New York serves as the Chair of the G-77 on climate change. During some of the Kyoto Protocol negotiations, the Chairs of the G-77 were: the Philippines (1995); Costa Rica (1996); and the United Republic of Tanzania (1997). The Group operates according to a consensus rule. Without consensus, i.e. all countries within this group agreeing, no common position is articulated. Given the wide variety of interests that the G-77 encompasses, however, it has been common for individual parties and groups also to speak during the Kyoto Protocol negotiations, even when there was a common position. G-77 symbolizes the North–South divide, with G-77 seeing climate change as really an issue about development. Two major concerns are articulated by this group: first, that poor countries' development will be hindered by having to reduce emissions, and, second, that carbon trade be allowed as a way of boosting income to developing countries.

## AOSIS

The Alliance of Small Island States was formed in 1990 during the Second World Climate Conference to represent the interests of low-lying and small island countries that are particularly vulnerable to sea-level rise. It comprises some 43 states, most of whom are also members of the G-77. This group has regularly spoken at the Protocol negotiations, often but not always through its Chair (Samoa, for most of the negotiations), though individual countries also intervened. The AOSIS position has always been to get the tightest control on global emissions as their countries seem to be most at threat from the impacts of global warming.

## JUSSCANNZ

This group of Non-EU OECD (Organization for Economic Cooperation and Development) acted as a loose information-sharing coalition during the Kyoto Protocol negotiations, without any coordinated positions. JUSSCANNZ stands for Japan, USA (who subsequently left the negotiations), Switzerland, Canada, Australia, Norway, and New Zealand. Iceland and other OECD countries, such as Mexico, often attended group meetings. The over-arching concern of

JUSSCANNZ has always been the cost of tackling climate change. The group is, however, split. Japan, New Zealand, Norway, and Iceland already enjoy a high energy efficiency and/or an energy mix dominated by low carbon sources. The greenhouse gas emissions per unit of GDP and per capita are, therefore, much lower than the OECD average, so their main concern is the cost of abatement. The second group is Australia, Canada, and the USA – the so-called new world countries – who face very different national circumstances with relatively low energy efficiency and an energy mix dominated by fossil fuels, growing populations, and large geographical areas, all of which lead to high emissions per unit of GDP and per capita. These countries' main concern is the cost of mitigating climate change because of the cost of changing their energy-intensive infrastructure.

## EU

The European Union has maintained a coordinated position on climate change, usually speaking through its Presidency, which rotates every six months. For example, during the Protocol negotiations the following countries have presided over the EU: Spain (late 1995), France (early 1996), Ireland (late 1996), Netherlands (early 1997), and Luxembourg (late 1997). It has been rare for individual EU states to speak during the Kyoto Protocol negotiations. The EU has a very similar split in its members to JUSSCANNZ, with both high and low energy-efficient economies. The consensus view of the EU has been to position itself as the environmental leader, with the attempt to advocate cuts as high as 15%. The EU rationale has been that any negotiated reduction could then be apportioned between the EU countries, depending on their development. This position has been greatly aided by both the UK and Germany experiencing a significant downturn in greenhouse emissions. In the UK this was done by replacing coal with gas, while Germany's downturn was due to updating and cleaning up the inefficient industries of former East Germany. However, the internal divisions within the EU and its cumbersome internal decision-making procedures make it a frustrating negotiating partner.

## OPEC

OPEC, the Organization of Petroleum Exporting Countries, regularly informally coordinated their positions in the climate change negotiations but have never spoken as a united group. The central position of this group is the protection of their main economic export, oil, and prevention of any treaty that undermines the significant usage of fossil fuels.

## African Group

The African Group is a formal regional group under the UN system, but it has only sometimes intervened during the negotiations. More often, countries within this group have spoken for themselves or through the coordinating role of the G-77. The African Group has been used mainly for ceremonial statements.

## ENGOs

ENGOs is short for Environmental Non-Governmental Organizations and though not homogeneous they had a relatively united view on climate change. They universally accepted the science of climate change and its possible impact, and campaigned for strong commitments on the part of governments and business to address the problem.

However, there are significant differences among the ENGOs regarding specific issues in the negotiations, particularly the possibility of emissions trading. The split can be seen in terms of reflecting a cultural difference between the new and old worlds. For example, Greenpeace International, based in Amsterdam, is strongly opposed to emissions trading while Brazilian Friends of the Earth are strongly supportive of it.

## BINGOs

Business and Industry Non-Governmental Organizations (BINGOs) were another powerful lobby at the Kyoto Protocol negotiations. However, unlike the ENGOs, they are a diverse and loose-knit group, with three main sub-groups. At the more progressive end of the spectrum lie 'green' business, including the 'sunrise' renewable energy industries and insurance companies, who recognized climate change as a potential business opportunity and urged decisive action on the part of governments. The middle ground was occupied by a group which accepted the science of climate change but called for a prudent, cautious approach to mitigation. At the other extreme are the fossil-fuel, mostly US-based industries such as the Global Climate Coalition. These were known as the grey BINGOs or the carbon club, who supported only the weakest action on climate change, stressing the economic costs and scientific uncertainties, echoing the editorials and bylines of most US newspapers and the British *Times* (see Chapter 2). Some of these BINGOs openly opposed the negotiations. Most notable was the Climate Council, a US-based lobby group run by Don Pearlman, a partner in a Washington law firm, which is widely believed to be a front for the

> fossil-fuel and energy interests in the USA. They have
> worked with OPEC states to block progress in both the IPCC
> and the climate change negotiations.

The box above outlines some of the major players at the Kyoto
Protocol negotiations. What is important when considering these
groups' views on global warming and climate change is to see how
each of these players fits on the global warming belief chart (see
Figure 11 and Chapter 3). It is interesting that despite all these
different views, a study by Joanna Depledge at University College
London showed that management of the Kyoto Protocol
negotiations was good, despite the size and the ambition of these
talks. She also provides some key lessons which could be used to
increase the effectiveness of any multilateral negotiations, and
ensure that the process is strengthened as it continues in the future.
These include the importance of having a single strong and efficient
presiding officer or negotiation chair and secretariat team
throughout the negotiating process, as these promote unity and
continuity. A balance between procedural equity/transparency and
efficiency must be maintained, because the negotiating process
must always continue to move forward, but at the same time the
participants must feel that it is a fair process. Bargaining and
cooperation should be promoted to accelerate the negotiations and
to prevent the tendency for discussion to stagnate. There must also
be strategies to overcome procedural obstructions, as these are
sometimes used as a stalling mechanism in negotiations. Finally,
Depledge suggests that an institutional memory should be
developed so that continued future negotiations have knowledge of
what has and has not worked in the past.

## Is the Kyoto Protocol flawed?

The first major flaw in the Kyoto Protocol, according to many, is
that it does not go far enough. The Kyoto Protocol currently

negotiated has cuts of emissions relative to 1990 levels of between 3 and 8% for just over half the developed world with no restrictions for the less-developed world, while scientists have suggested up to a 60% global cut is required to prevent major climatic change. Hence it is suggested that the Kyoto Protocol will do nothing to prevent global warming and is not significantly different from a business-as-usual situation; which is of course what many developed countries want in order to maintain their economy.

What even the most effective negotiations cannot deal with is withdrawal from the process. So the second major flaw in the Kyoto Protocol is the non-participation of the USA. It is, however, unsurprising that the USA withdrew from these climate change negotiations: US carbon dioxide emissions have already risen by 12% compared with 1990 levels and are predicted to rise by more than 30% by 2012 compared to 1990 levels. So if they had agreed to ratify the Kyoto Protocol, they would have had to cut their emissions by over a third, which successive Presidents have seen as a direct threat to the US economy and their chances of re-election. There is, however, a deeper divide between the USA and, for example, the EU. Many political commentators have referred to this as the transatlantic rift. Americans have historically tended not to see any source of democratic legitimacy higher than the constitutional nation-state. Therefore, any international organization only has legitimacy because the democratic majorities have handed up this legitimacy through a negotiated contractual process. Such legitimacy can be withdrawn at any time by the contracting parties. Europeans, by contrast, tend to believe democratic legitimacy flows from the will of an international community which is much larger than any individual nation-state. This international community hands down legitimacy to existing international institutions, which are seen as partially embodying the ideals and precepts of the international community. At the start of the 21st century the difference in approaches between the USA and other nation-states could not be more stark. Not only has the Bush administration withdrawn from the Kyoto Protocol negotiations, but it has failed to ratify the Rio pact on biodiversity, withdrawn from the anti-ballistics missile treaty, opposed the ban on landmines, opposed amendments to the biological warfare convention, opposed the setting up of an international criminal court, and sidelined the UN in the lead-up to the second Iraq war. This pattern of US unilateralism should not be seen as just a transitory problem reflecting the Bush administration but rather it shows the fundamental schism between the world-views of the USA and the rest of the Western world. This is not to say that either view is more or less valid. The problem is that 'future climate change' is a global concern, with causes and effects that go far beyond the boundaries of the nation-state. Rather like the revolution in the 1980s, when the geographical scope of environmental problems was enlarged to encompass the globe, a new 'global' geographical view of politics is required. Hence the climate change negotiations and related world trade talks are fundamentally flawed without the multilateral multi-nation-state approach. The USA is so important to both processes because of its economic size. Currently the US population is 280 million and has a GDP of $7 trillion, compared with the whole of Europe, which has 375 million people and a GDP of $10 trillion

## Cost of climate change and development issues

One of the major obstacles to dealing with the global warming problem is cost, or more importantly perception of cost. This problem is very rarely dealt with by the media or environmentalists but is the fundamental reason why the Kyoto Protocol may ultimately fail. Figure 33 estimates the cost in US dollars to the world in 2000 of five different economic scenarios. The business-as-usual case provides a value of the damage global warming will cause, about 4.8 trillion dollars – about half the GDP of the whole of the European Union. If some mitigating policies are included then this cost can be reduced in the optimal case to 4.6 trillion. However, if steps are taken to stabilize carbon dioxide emissions at the 1990s level, it would cost the world nearly double – $8.6 trillion, $1.6 trillion more than the GDP of the USA. It would be slightly cheaper to aim at preventing the global temperature rising above 2.5°C at $7.8 trillion. If we wanted to prevent global temperatures from rising above 1.5°C it would cost a staggering $37 trillion. These costs are astronomical and when dealing with the global warming issue one must be realistic about what the world can and cannot afford to do. Of course, all of these scenarios assume a steady change in climate change suggested by the GCMs and, of course, no account is taken of the possibility of abrupt climatic shifts. Another way of looking at all these huge figures is in terms of what the world earns. If we implement Kyoto or attempt to stabilize the effects of global warming, then the cost to the world could be as high as 2% of the world GDP. Now is this a lot of money? Well, it depends on how you look at it, as this amount is equivalent to worldwide annual spending on the military. Moreover, it has been pointed out that the world economy is predicted to grow by 2–3% over the next century, so dealing with global warming is cutting off the growth curve for one year. This would be like waiting until 2051 to enjoy the prosperity of 2050. And of course by that time the average world citizen will be twice as wealthy as they are now. So looked at this way, the cost worldwide of dealing with global warming seems to be quite reasonable.

The second consideration when investigating the cost of limiting global warming is the moral dilemma that this money could be spent elsewhere to relieve human suffering. For example, the current Kyoto Protocol, if implemented, would cost a minimum of $150 billion per year, while UNICEF estimates that just $70–80 billion per year could give all Third World inhabitants access to the basics like health, education, water, and sanitation. So global warming provides us with some major moral problems. Bjørn

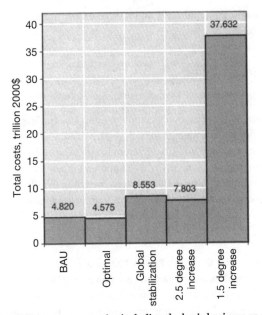

33. **Five different cost scenarios including the basic business-as-usual (BAU)**

Lomborg suggests that this connection between the resources used on global warming and aiding the Third World goes much deeper, because it will be the developing world that suffers most from the effects of global warming as they are least able to adapt. If we mitigate global warming, we are in fact helping future generations in the Third World. However, if we spent the same money but directly on the developing world, we would be helping the current inhabitants and thus their descendants. As we have seen that the average global citizen will be twice as well off by 2050, we have a real moral dilemma: do we help the more well-off inhabitants of the developing world a hundred years from now or do we help the poorer inhabitants of the present Third World? The proviso to this is that if we help the Third World to develop quickly now, will this accelerate global warming significantly and thus cost more in the long run?

## Emissions trading

One of the most controversial issues in the climate change negotiations is international carbon or emissions trading. It has support from countries in both G-77, JUSSCANNZ, and also many BINGOs and ENGOs from less-developed countries. It is seen by many as an essential component of any treaty which would include the USA. Others, including the EU and international ENGOs, see carbon trading as morally wrong. So compromise over this issue is in very short supply.

However, under the Kyoto Protocol national governments can issue shares of its agreed carbon emission reduction in the form of tradable certificates that show compliance with targets. Companies involved in energy and power production can then decide either to reduce their greenhouse gas emissions or purchase these certificates from another company with surplus permits. These permits are only issued once the company has exceeded its reduction target. By introducing this trading scenario it allows the cheapest cost of reducing carbon emission to be found. For example, companies which are already energy/carbon-efficient would find it very expensive to reduce emissions by a fixed amount compared with a more inefficient company. So not only does trading produce the least-cost option but encourages development of innovative abatement technologies, i.e. low carbon emission technologies. This is compared to the carbon tax option, whereby companies would be charged a fixed tax per tonne of carbon emitted, which provides an incentive only to adjust production levels, which generally benefits neither business nor society.

In the USA emissions trading has already played a central role in reducing sulphur dioxide and nitrous oxides, the primary component of acid rain. This has been highly successful. The Clean Air Act of 1990 required electrical utilities to lower their emissions of these pollutants by 8.5 million tonnes compared with 1980 levels. Initial estimates in 1989 suggested it would cost $7.4 billion; a report in 1998 based on actual compliance data suggested it had cost less than $1 billion.

The world's first legislative-backed national greenhouse gas market is the UK Emissions Trading Scheme, which opened for business in April 2002. A European-wide trading scheme is expected to begin in 2005 with at least 5,000 companies in Europe facing emissions control. The United Nations Environment Programme predicts that by the end of the first compliance period of the Kyoto Protocol, 2008–12, over $2 trillion will have been traded. This is because countries failing to reach the first set of targets by 2012 will have to add the shortfall to the next commitment period, plus a 30% penalty. They will also be excluded from carbon trading and be forced to take corrective measures at home. Contrary to initial beliefs, participation in emissions trading has not increased cost, and a number of oil companies have found that it has given them a cost advantage over their competitors.

This is still, however, a long way from the carbon credit system that many less-developed countries want. This would involve industrial nations buying carbon credits on the international market. These international carbon credits would be generated by any country by reforestation or changing agricultural practice, which means more carbon is stored in the biosphere compared with 1990 levels, or by lowering industrial emissions, because, as we have seen above, it is much more cost-effective to reduce emissions from inefficient industries, which are common in less-developed countries, than efficient industries. Less-developed countries see this as an essential way of generating money and accelerating development while making sure emissions are reduced. Some see this as the only way the USA could afford to comply with the Kyoto Protocol, if and when they decide to rejoin.

## Local initiatives

Global warming does not have to be dealt with solely at the international level and there are a lot of good examples of initiatives at the local level. So while national governments have been taking time to try to thrash out a global deal, local governments and individuals have been pushing forward their own solutions for the last ten years. The driving force behind a lot of these efforts is the Agenda 21 document accepted at the United Nations Conference on Environment and Development at Rio de Janeiro in June 1992. This document stresses the participation of both local agencies and individuals in developing solutions to environmental change, development, and sustainability. Most local authorities have policies addressing the key issues in the Agenda 21 document. An example of this comes from New Hampshire in the USA: there Governor Jeanne Shaheen has facilitated the meeting of local business, government, and the environment sector to brainstorm solutions to cut greenhouse gases within the state. The major problem was that, in the past, companies who had voluntarily reduced air pollution had been punished because, with the introduction of the 1990 federal Clean Air Act Amendments, companies who had already started to clean up their act were given stricter emission reduction targets than companies who were dirtier. Through the gathering of interested parties in New Hampshire, it was decided that the state would support companies that made voluntary reductions, and this was done through a registry of all the reductions made in greenhouse gas emissions. This collective action has resulted in state legislation which was passed in 1999 and has had many benefits; one immediate effect was a significant improvement in local air quality. These innovative solutions were also noticed by Wisconsin and California and similar legal processes were completed there in 2000. Moreover, Wisconsin was the first state in the USA to complete a state-wide climate action cost study. They found that by implementing solutions that cost nothing or even saved money (e.g. energy efficiency measures) they could create over 8,000 new jobs in the state, save nearly half a billion dollars, raise Wisconsin state's gross product, and reduce over 75 million tonnes of carbon dioxide emissions.

Another level on which global warming can be dealt with is that of the nation-state and there are many examples of individual countries taking the lead to cut their own fossil-fuel emissions. One shining light is Iceland. Currently it obtains 99% of its electricity from geysers and hydroelectric dams. But it imports 850,000 tonnes of oil to meet 35% of its energy needs, used mainly for transport, fishing, and metal production. This gives Iceland one of the higher per capita carbon emission rates in the world. However, they are politically committed to becoming the world's first hydrogen economy, cutting greenhouse emissions to zero in the next 30 years. Their vision is to develop the technology to split water into hydrogen and oxygen and use the hydrogen as a fuel, hence producing no harmful greenhouse gases. This example shows that when there is a political will and conviction, something can be done about our obsession with a fossil-fuel economy. But you must also consider that there are major problems with a hydrogen economy, as there are great dangers from leaks and the need to maintain the gas under high pressures. Moreover, energy is required in the first place to split water to extract the hydrogen which will require fossil fuels. So the 'hydrogen' economy is not the global solution to global warming.

# Chapter 9
# What are the alternatives?

Until a few decades ago it was generally thought that significant large-scale global and regional climate changes occurred gradually over a timescale of many centuries or millennia, hence the climate shifts were assumed to be scarcely perceptible during a human lifetime. The tendency of climate to change abruptly throughout human history has been one of the most surprising outcomes of the study of past climates. There is good evidence that some of the most pronounced climate changes involved a regional change of up to 5°C in mean annual temperature within a few decades, or even just a few years. These decadal-timescale transitions would presumably have been quite noticeable to humans living at such times. It is known that one of these short, cold, arid periods about 4,300 years ago had a profound effect on classical civilizations. Many of these civilizations could not adapt to the climate changes and collapsed, including the Old Kingdom in Egypt; the Akkadian Empire in Mesopotamia; the Early Bronze Age societies of Anatolia, Greece, and Israel; the Indus valley civilization in India; the Hilmand civilization in Afghanistan; and the Hongshan culture of China. It has also been shown that climate deterioration, particularly a succession of severe droughts in Central America during the Medieval Cold Period, prompted the collapse of the classic period of the Mayan civilization. Moreover, the rise and fall of the Incas can be linked to alternating wet and dry periods, which favoured the coastal and highland cultures of Ecuador and Peru. We know,

| | Very Low | | | | Higher | Risks from Future Large-Scale Discontinuities |
| | | | | | | |
| | Positive or Negative Market Impacts; Majority of People Adversely Affected | | | | Net Negative in All Metrics | Aggregate Impacts |
| | | | | | | |
| | Negative for Some Regions | | | Negative for Most Regions | | Distribution of Impacts |
| | | | | | | |
| | Increase | | | | Large Increase | Risks from Extreme Climate Events |
| | | | | | | |
| | Risks to Some | | | | Risks to Many | Risks to Unique and Threatened Systems |

-0.6    0    1    2    3    4    5

← Past    Future →

34. Climate change risks with increasing global temperatures

however, that humans can survive a whole range of climates. The collapse of these urban civilizations, then, is not about climate making an area inhospitable; rather the society was unable to adapt to the climate changes, particularly changes in water resources. For example, for the Mayan civilization to have survived, it would have needed to recognize its vulnerability to long-term water shortages and should have developed a more flexible approach, i.e. developing new water sources, developing new means of conserving water, and prioritizing water use in times of shortage.

So climate change is an external pressure on a society, but it is the structure of the society, particularly how flexible it is, that determines whether it survives or not. This is an important lesson. As the weight of evidence strongly suggests that global warming will cause climate change, we have to make sure that our global society and economy are flexible enough to deal with these changes. The IPCC 2001 *Report on Impacts, Adaptation and Vulnerability* provides a very useful diagram of key societal impacts and at what increased global temperatures they may occur (Figure 34). This is a valuable management tool as it shows how these five reasons for concern may vary in the 21st century. It is on this risk scale that we need to judge the cost of adaptation and mitigation versus the various regional and global impacts.

## Adaptation and mitigation

The most sensible approach to preventing the worst effects of global warming would be to cut carbon dioxide emissions. Scientists believe a cut of between 60 and 80% is required to avoid the worst effects of global warming. But many have argued that the cost of significant cuts in fossil-fuel use would severely affect the global economy, preventing the rapid development of the Third World. The ratification of the Kyoto Protocol at the Bonn meeting in July 2001 will only amount to a cut of between 1 and 3% for the

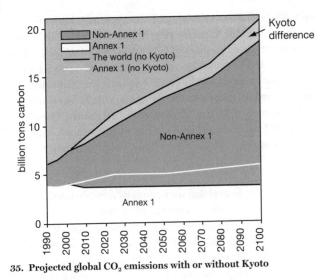

**35. Projected global CO$_2$ emissions with or without Kyoto**

developed world (Annex 1), while the developing world (non-Annex 1) will continue to increase their emissions (see Figure 35). So the second major aim of the IPCC is to study and report on the potential sensitivity, adaptability, and vulnerability of each national environment and socio-economic system because if we can predict what the impacts of global warming are likely to be, then national governments can take action to mitigate the effects. For example, if flooding is going to become more prevalent in Britain, then damage to property and loss of life can be prevented with strict new laws which limit building on flood plains and vulnerable coasts.

The IPCC believes there are six reasons why we must adapt to climate change. (1) Climate change cannot be avoided; (2) anticipatory and precautionary adaptation is more effective and less costly than forced last-minute emergency fixes; (3) climate change may be more rapid and more pronounced than current estimates suggest, and unexpected events, as we have seen, are more than just possible; (4) immediate benefits can be gained from better adaptation to climate variability and extreme atmospheric events: for example, with the hurricane risk, strict building laws and better evacuation practices would need to be implemented; (5) immediate benefits can also be gained by removing maladaptive policies and practices, for example, building on flood plains and vulnerable coastlines; and (6) climate change brings opportunities as well as threats. Future benefits can result from climate change. The IPCC has provided many ideas of how one can adapt to climate change; an example is given in Figure 36 of how countries can adapt to predicted sea rise.

The major threat from global warming is its unpredictability. Humanity can live in almost any extreme of climate from deserts to the Arctic, but only when we can predict what the extremes of the weather will be. So adaptation is really the key to dealing with the global warming problem, but it must start now, as infrastructure changes can take up to 50 years to implement. For example, if you want to change land use, e.g. building better sea defences or returning farmland back to natural wetlands in a particular area, it can take up to 20 years to research and plan the appropriate changes. It can then take another ten years for the full consultative and legal processes; an example of this is the time it has taken to agree a strategy to expand London airports. It can take another ten years to implement these changes and a following decade for the natural restoration to take place (see Figure 37).

The other problem is that adaptation requires money to be invested now; many countries just do not have the money and elsewhere in the world people do not want to pay more taxes to protect themselves in the future as most people live for today. This is, of course, despite the fact that all of the adaptations discussed will in the long term save money for the local area, the country, and the world; we as a global society still have a very short-term view, usually measured in a few years between successive governments.

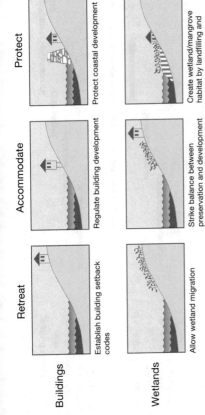

**Retreat**     **Accommodate**     **Protect**

**Buildings**

Establish building setback codes     Regulate building development     Protect coastal development

**Wetlands**

Allow wetland migration     Strike balance between preservation and development     Create wetland/mangrove habitat by landfilling and planting

**Crops**

Relocate agricultural production     Switch to aquaculture     Protect agricultural land

36. **Model response strategies for future sea-level rise**

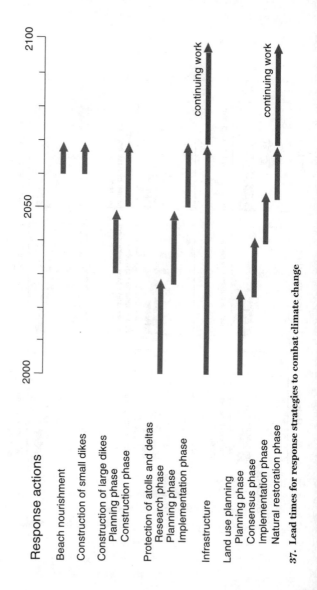

37. Lead times for response strategies to combat climate change

# Technofixes, can we fix global warming?

How can we deal with global warming? We have seen that governments are slowly getting their act together to reduce carbon dioxide emission; however, there are concerns over how much this will cost. There has therefore been a lot of interest in 'alternatives' or 'technofixes' for solving the problem of global warming. There are four main areas of technofixes:

1. $CO_2$ removal from industrial processes can contribute substantially to a reduction in atmospheric $CO_2$; however, further research and development is required to improve the performance and their application of these methods within the concepts of sustainable development.

2. We can use less energy and thus produce less carbon dioxide. It is feasible to improve energy efficiency by 50% on average over the next three decades, although this will require tough policy measures, like the introduction of a high-energy or carbon tax. An example is that efficiency in power generation can be increased by 60% using advanced technologies in the field of gas turbines and fuel cells.

3. There are renewable/alternative energy sources, i.e. energy sources which do not produce a net amount of carbon dioxide in the atmosphere. Most promising in the short term is biomass, which by the year 2020 could produce a third of the global energy. When the biomass is growing it absorbs carbon dioxide from the atmosphere which is only returned when it is burnt as a fuel and thus there is no net increase in atmospheric carbon dioxide. Most promising for the long term is solar energy, while wind power is thought to be an excellent intermediate solution, particularly in countries such as the UK, where sunlight cannot be guaranteed. Many countries are also discussing renewing their nuclear programmes as a non-carbon-emission energy source, but problems of safety and dumping nuclear waste still remain the main objections.

Alternative energies are no longer the remit of the environmental NGOs; with the exception of some US oil companies, with Exxon/ Mobil (Esso in Europe) top of the list, most of the rest of the global business community is reacting rapidly to the need for different energy sources. In the last five years, companies like Ford and oil companies like BP and Shell have begun to pour billions of dollars into researching new technologies. Wind power is now mainstream, solar power is in rapid development, hybrid cars are on the roads. Cars that run on fuel cells, hydrogen, and compressed air are no longer pipe dreams.

4. There is the possibility of removing carbon dioxide from the atmosphere either by growing new forests or by stimulating the ocean to take up more. This idea is discussed in greater detail below in the iron hypothesis section.

All of these technologies make sense and a combination of them could be used to combat global warming, although they each have their drawbacks. Removal of carbon dioxide during industrial processes is tricky and costly, because not only does the $CO_2$ need to be removed, but it must be stored somewhere as well. Removal and storage costs could be somewhere between \$20 and \$50 per tonne $CO_2$. This would cause a 35% to 100% increase in power production costs. However, recovered $CO_2$ does not all need to be stored; some may be utilized in enhanced oil recovery, the food industry, chemical manufacturing (producing soda ash, urea, and methanol), and the metal-processing industries. $CO_2$ can also be applied to the production of construction material, solvents, cleaning compounds and packaging, and in waste-water treatment. But in reality, most of the carbon dioxide captured from industrial processes would have to be stored. It has been estimated that theoretically two-thirds of the $CO_2$ formed from the combustion of the world's total oil and gas reserves could be stored in the corresponding reservoirs. Other estimates indicate storage of 90–400 GtC in natural gas fields alone and another 90 GtC in aquifers. Oceans could also be used to dispose of the carbon dioxide. Suggestions have included storage by hydrate dumping, i.e. if you mix carbon dioxide and water at high pressure and low temperatures it creates a solid or hydrate which is heavier than the surrounding water and thus drops to the bottom. This hydrate is very similar to the methane hydrates discussed Chapter 7.

The major problem with all of these methods of storage is safety. Carbon dioxide is a very dangerous gas because it is heavier than air and causes suffocation. An important example of this was in 1986, when a tremendous explosion of $CO_2$ from Lake Nyos, in the west of Cameroon, killed more than 1,700 people and livestock up to 25 km away. Though similar disasters had previously occurred, never had so many people and animals been asphyxiated on such a scale in a single brief event. What we now believe happened was that dissolved $CO_2$ from the nearby volcano seeped from springs beneath the lake and was trapped in deep water by the weight of water above. In 1986 there was an avalanche which mixed up the lake waters, resulting in an explosive overturn of the whole lake, and all the trapped carbon dioxide was released in one go, proving that the storage of carbon dioxide is very difficult and potentially lethal. With ocean storage there is the added complication that the ocean circulates, so whatever carbon dioxide you dump, some of it will eventually return. Moreover, scientists are very uncertain about the environmental effects on the ocean ecosystems. At the moment, therefore, we have no estimates of the amount of $CO_2$ that can be safely stored.

Ultimately, a combination of improved energy efficiency and alternative energy is the solution to global warming. From the safety and environmental perspective, the storage of carbon dioxide either underground and/or in the ocean is really not feasible, however helpful this would be in the short term.

# Iron hypothesis

As we have seen, global warming is constantly on the political agenda, even if politicians do not like to mention it. The problem, however, is that cutting carbon dioxide emissions has a huge economic price tag. So scientists and politicians are always looking for a quick fix or a 'technofix' for global warming. The late Professor John Martin has put forward one of the most controversial ideas yet. He suggested that many of the world's oceans are under-producing. This is because of the lack of vital nutrients, the most important of which is iron which allows plants to grow in the surface waters. Marine plants need minute quantities of iron and without it they cannot grow. In most oceans enough iron-rich dust gets blown in from the land, but it seems that large areas of the Pacific and Southern Ocean do not receive much dust and thus are barren of iron. So it has been suggested that we could fertilize the ocean with iron. This would stimulate marine productivity. The extra photosynthesis would convert more surface-water carbon dioxide into organic matter. When the organisms die the organic matter drops to the bottom of the ocean, taking with it and storing the extra carbon. The reduced surface-water carbon dioxide is replenished by carbon dioxide from the atmosphere. So, in short, fertilizing the world's oceans could help to remove atmospheric carbon dioxide and store it in deep-sea sediments. Experiments at sea have shown that the amount of iron required is huge, and as soon as you stop adding the extra iron, much of this stored carbon dioxide is released. There is also another, darker, side to this iron hypothesis. It seems that because of industrialization and also worldwide land-use changes, there is about 150% more dust in the atmosphere than 200 years ago. This extra dust has increased the ocean's ability to take carbon dioxide out of the atmosphere. So our dirty atmosphere is literally helping us against global warming. However, under the Kyoto Protocol countries are encouraged to start expanding forests and preventing soil erosion to draw carbon dioxide out of the atmosphere. This will ultimately lead to a decrease in dust. Calculations by Dr Andrew Ridgwell at the

University of British Columbia (Canada) and myself suggest that a significant proportion of the extra carbon dioxide stored on land under the Kyoto Protocol could be returned to the atmosphere, because the decrease in overall dust will start to limit iron in the ocean and thus productivity. The reduced ability of the ocean to suck out atmospheric carbon dioxide will, over hundreds of years, wipe out the short-term gain from planting all those new forests.

# Chapter 10
# Conclusion

Global warming is one of the few scientific theories which makes us examine the whole basis of modern society. It is a theory that has politicians arguing, sets nations against each other, queries individual choices of lifestyle and ultimately asks the questions about humanity's relationship with the rest of the planet. There is very little doubt that global warming will change our climate in the next century; our best estimates suggest an average temperature increase of 1.4–5.8°C, a sea-level rise in the order of a metre, significant changes in weather patterns, and more extreme climate events. This is not, however, the end of the world, as envisaged by many environmentalists in the late 1980s and early 1990s, but does produce some major challenges for our global society, the most important of which are the moral dilemmas that global warming has precipitated. First, how do we ensure that the Third World develops as rapidly as possible, while preventing a massive explosion in production of carbon dioxide and other greenhouse gases? Second, is the question of whether the money we plan to spend on stabilizing global warming, $8 trillion or 2% of the World's GDP, to protect future generations is better spent on alleviating current global human suffering? Ultimately, 2% of the World's GDP is a very small cost if we can ensure that the world economy continues to grow by 2–3% per year over the next century as predicted. So ultimately global warming is an issue of morals and global economics.

So what are the solutions to global warming? As we have seen, it is unlikely that global politics will solve global warming. Technofixes are dangerous or cause problems as bad as the ones they are aimed at fixing. Even the idea of using energy more efficiently seems rather inadequate when there are another five and half billion people in the world aspiring to have the energy use enjoyed by the Western world. So the ultimate solution is for humanity to develop cheap and clean energy production, as all economic development is based on ever-increasing energy usage. Though great strides forward have been made in alternative energies, it seems unlikely that these will produce energy on the scale we require in the next few decades. As I am a great believer in humanity's adaptability, I am sure these will be available before the end of the century. But a considerable increase in investment is required if we are to convert to renewable energy by the end of the century; for example, current US investment in renewable energy is just $200 million per year. Even if renewable energy technology does become available, there is no guarantee that it would be made affordable to all nations, since we live in a world where even life-saving drugs are costed to achieve maximum profit. Nor is there any guarantee that if we had unlimited free energy it would prevent us from continuing to abuse the planet. Paul Ehrlich at Stanford University, commenting on the possibility of unlimited clean energy from cold fusion, suggested it would be 'like giving a machine gun to an idiot child'.

We cannot pin all our hopes on clean energy technology, nor our ability to use it wisely, so we must prepare for the worst and adapt. If implemented now, a lot of the costs and damage that could be caused by changing climate can be mitigated. This requires nations and regions to plan for the next 50 years, something that most societies are unable to do because of the very short-term nature of politics. So global warming challenges the very way we organize our society. Not only does it challenge the concept of the nation-state versus global responsibility, but the short-term vision of our political leaders. To answer the question of what we can do about global warming, we must change some of the basic rules of our society to allow us to adopt a much more global and long-term approach.

I leave you with thoughts of redesigning our global community with the excellent words of Professor Wally Broecker of Columbia University (USA):

'Climate is an ill-tempered beast, and we are poking it with sticks.'

38. Is global warming all bad?

# Further reading

Adams, J., (1995) *Risk*, UCL Press.

*Climate Change 2001: The Scientific Basis*, Contribution of Working Group I to the Third Assessment Report of the Intergovernmental Panel on Climate Change (IPCC), Houghton *et al.* (eds) Cambridge University Press.

*Climate Change 2001: Impacts, Adaptation, and Vulnerability*, Contribution of Working Group II to the Third Assessment Report of the Intergovernmental Panel on Climate Change (IPCC), McCarthy *et al.* (eds) Cambridge University Press.

*Climate Change 2001: Mitigation*, Contribution of Working Group III to the Third Assessment Report of the Intergovernmental Panel on Climate Change (IPCC), Metz *et al.* (eds) Cambridge University Press.

*Climate Change impacts on the United States, Overview*, National Assessment Synthesis Team (2000) Cambridge University Press.

de Carvalho, A. S. (2002) 'Climate in the New: The British Press and the Discursive Construction of the Greenhouse Effect', Ph.D. thesis, UCL, University of London.

Depledge, J. J. (2001) 'Managing the Performance: Lessons from the Organization of the Kyoto Protocol Negotiations', Ph.D. thesis, UCL, University of London.

Drake, F. (2000) *Global Warming: The Science of Climate Change*, Arnold.

Gribbin, J. (1990) *Hothouse Earth: The Greenhouse Effect and Gaia*, Grove Weidenfeld.

Harvey, D. (2000) *Global Warming: The Hard Science*, Prentice Hall.

Houghton, J. T. (1997) *Global Warming : The Complete Briefing* (2nd edn) Cambridge University Press. (Note that the 3rd edn will be published in 2004.)

Lawton, J. H., Marotzke, J., March, R., and McCave, I. N. (eds) (2003) *Abrupt Climate Change: Evidence, Mechanism and Implications* (14 papers) Philosophical Transactions of the Royal Society of London, series A, 361/1810.

Leggett, J. K. (2001) *The Carbon War: Global Warming and the End of the Oil Era*, Routledge.

Lomborg, B. (2001) *The Skeptical Environmentalist: Measuring the Real State of the World*, Cambridge University Press.

National Research Council (2002) *Abrupt Climate Change: Inevitable Surprises*, National Academy Press.

Robinson, K. S. (2004) *Forty Signs of Rain* (novel which has some excellent insights into how climate change science operates) Harper Collins.

Weart, S. R. (2003) *The Discovery of Global Warming, New Histories of Science, Technology, and Medicine*, Harvard University Press.

Wilson, R. C. L., Drury, S. A., and Chapman, J. L. (2003) *The Great Ice Age: Climate Change and Life*, Routledge.

realclimate.org

http://www.pages.unibe.ch

http://www.climateark.org

http://www.ipcc.ch

# Index

Index

Index

Visit the
# VERY SHORT INTRODUCTIONS
Web site

# www.oup.co.uk/vsi

➤ **Information** about all published titles

➤ News of **forthcoming books**

➤ **Extracts** from the books, including titles not yet published

➤ **Reviews** and views

➤ **Links** to other **web sites** and main OUP web page

➤ Information about **VSIs in translation**

➤ **Contact** the editors

➤ **Order** other **VSIs** on-line

# Expand your collection of
# VERY SHORT INTRODUCTIONS

# DARWIN
## A Very Short Introduction
Jonathan Howard

Darwin's theory of evolution, which implied that our ancestors were apes, caused a furore in the scientific world and beyond when *The Origin of Species* was published in 1859. Arguments still rage about the implications of his evolutionary theory, and scepticism about the value of Darwin's contribution to knowledge is widespread. In this analysis of Darwin's major insights and arguments, Jonathan Howard reasserts the importance of Darwin's work for the development of modern science and culture.

> 'Jonathan Howard has produced an intellectual *tour de force*, a classic in the genre of popular scientific exposition which will still be read in fifty years' time'
>
> **Times Literary Supplement**

www.oup.co.uk/isbn/0-19-285454-2